It is what it is.

— Mayor Frank Jackson

Gray & Company, Publishers

www.grayco.com

ISBN 978-1-938441-07-3

Printed in the United States of America

1

Contents

CHAPTER ONE

Housing Hope: Does increased demand for residential real estate loans signal Cleveland's continued economic recovery?

CHAPTER TWO

Reading, Writing and Robbery: How Cleveland's well-intended school voucher plan went so horribly astray.

CHAPTER THREE

Spanning The Chasm: A brief history of Cleveland's more than 300 bridges, past and present.

CHAPTER FOUR

Winds of Change: Examining Cleveland's opportunity to be at the forefront of offshore wind energy.

CHAPTER FIVE

The "G" Word: Was the gentrification of Ohio City worth compromising the area's rich history

CHAPTER SIX

The Pasta Masta': An intimate look at the life of Cleveland's own Angelo Vitantonio (1876–1934), inventor of the first hand-cranked pasta machine.

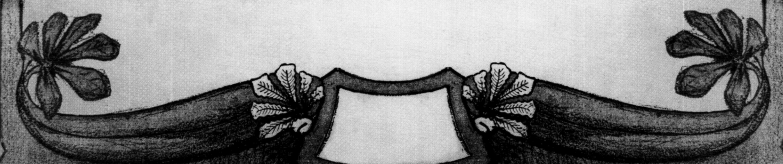

STOP! Don't move. Just let me look at you for a second. My God, you look beautiful. Turn around. All the way around. Yep. There it is. How did I get so lucky?

Look, I don't care how you ended up here reading the introduction to my regionally themed comedy/picture book. The important thing is that you're here. And we're together. And we will be together for the next contractually obligated 100+ pages. So let's just appreciate this moment.

When Cleveland publishing company Gray & Company contacted me to ask if I'd be interested in writing this book, my first thought was, wait, Cleveland has a publishing company?

So I Googled them to make sure I wasn't getting involved in yet another Internet scam. (If anyone runs into a Nigerian Prince named Emeka Shangari, tell him he still owes me the thousand I sent to liberate him from his captors *and* the emerald mine he promised me!)

It turns out that Gray is in fact a real publisher that puts out lots of real Cleveland-themed books. But most of them are either about local ghosts, little kids who got kidnapped from suburbs in the 1980s or Omar Vizquel. So I wasn't sure that my style of whatever-it-is-that-I-do would be appreciated or even tolerated in such company.

They assured me that they trusted my creative process implicitly and informed me that I would have free reign to do whatever I wanted. So I immediately sent them my first draft: 100 pictures of my donger wearing different kinds of hats. (The sombrero was my favorite, but the top hat made it look both fancy and more "extensive")

They then slightly altered their original statement and said that I could give them anything "within reason," which is dangerously subjective, and they gave me the following additional parameters: It had to be about Cleveland and it had to be at least 100 pages long.

And I feel as though I have accomplished just that. What follows is a sloppy, disjointed amalgamation of random jokes, rambling essays, easy digs, transcribed Internet videos, and pictures, lots of space-eating pictures!

Now, I don't pretend to know much about big city book-writin'. My artistic experience is rooted predominantly in stand up, sketch comedy, Internet videos and karaoke. So I probably won't win a Grammy for this, or whatever. But it was fun to work on. And I had a good time wandering around the city

looking for different things to make fun of.

I catch some flack from people sometimes about how hard I rag on Cleveland, and that's understandable. People are protective of their city, and I get that. But let me assure you that my joking comes from a place of love. I wouldn't pick on this city if I didn't care about it and if I didn't think we could take it. Cleveland is like a little brother to me who I'm allowed to make fun of because we're family and that's what we do. But if some asshole from Indianapolis mouths off about it, I do not hesitate to set him straight.

Cleveland has a rich history and a promising future. I truly believe that. It's full of great stuff to see and do and the most genuine people I have ever known. But talking about that good stuff isn't funny, and I have some space to fill here. So let's all give Parma some shit for a while instead.

Stay Cleveland Strong!

— Mike

FOREWORD

BY THE CLEVELAND TOURISM BOARD

We at The Cleveland Tourism Board would like to start by saying that we do not approve of Mike Polk or anything that he says or does. We do not consider any aspect of his "work" amusing or impressive. It is the basest of humor aimed at the broadest of audiences and the fact that it has found any sort of minor following is a sad testament to the current state of our society.

That said, when Mr. Polk asked us to write the foreword for his Cleveland "humor" book, we saw it as an opportunity to rebut in advance what are certain to be the many unfounded criticisms and cheap digs at our city that we assume this publication will contain.

We stress that we can only assume this fact, as we refuse to subject ourselves to the punishment of reading his drivel. But because of the lack of originality Polk has displayed in the past, we are all but certain that we know what it contains.

If you are just browsing through the first few pages of this book and have not yet committed to purchasing it from whatever Adult Mart or gas station that has for some reason agreed to stock it, we at The Cleveland Tourism Board strongly suggest that you put it down and purchase a more positive Cleveland-themed publication. For example, check out Neil Zurcher's most recent One Tank Trip book where he goes to Holmes County to visit Amish country and learns how to make faceless dolls.

But most importantly, do not buy this book or support anything that Mike Polk does. He's a shameless, bitter, talentless charlatan who is exploiting Clevelanders' insecurities for cheap laughs and financial gain, and he needs to be stopped. We wish him nothing but failure and sadness, and we truly hope that he simply disappears and continues his empty existence somewhere far away from our grand city.

Fuck Mike Polk Jr.

All that said, please be sure to visit The Cleveland Botanical Garden's new "Madagascar Madness!" display, celebrating the unique flora and fauna of this biodiversity hotspot. And don't forget about this year's "Taste of Cleveland," featuring food samples from more than a dozen area restaurants and musical performances by Candlebox and Queensryche!

And again, fuck Mike Polk Jr.

The Cleveland Tourism Board

THE ORIGIN OF CLE~A~VELAND:
WHY DID THIS HAPPEN?

Let us begin at the beginning. Where do we come from? How was Cleveland founded? Through some painstaking research into our city's archives (Wikipedia), here is a quick rundown of how Cleveland came to be.

It's a pretty common misconception that Cleveland was founded in 1977, the year of my birth. But this is just one of those old wives' tales I started that has yet to gain traction. In actuality, Cleveland was founded in 1796 by General Moses Cleaveland, who, as you can tell by his picture, originated the long-standing Cleveland citizen tradition of being grim and unattractive.

General Cleaveland's expedition coasted along the shore of Lake Erie and landed at the mouth of the Cuyahoga River on July 22, 1796, where he was the first person to utter the now common phrase, "What is that smell?" Despite this, he declared it to be as good a place as any to found a city, most likely because he was tired of rowing.

A delegation of Mohawk nation and Seneca tribe Indians opposed Cleaveland's claim to the land, citing the weak argument that they themselves had lived there for thousands of years. After tense negotiations, the tribes waived their rights to the territory upon the receipt of beads and whiskey valued at $1,200. They then quickly retreated to their dugout canoes and screamed, "No take backs!" in their savage tongue. To this day, Native Americans still laugh about the lopsided nature of the deal, particularly when walking past the vacant Galleria Mall.

The new inhabitants named the place Cleaveland, in honor of their chief. Somewhere along the way, we inadvertently dropped the first "A" in the name of our city, not only insulting our founder with the misspelling but getting our region's educational system off to a terribly prophetic start.

One little-known, true and hilarious fact is that Moses Cleaveland went home to Connecticut after the 1796 expedition and never returned to Ohio or the city that bears his name. Ever. Even our founder got the hell out of here. He didn't last a year. This is also the first recorded example of "white flight" from the city.

What follows is the exchange between Moses Cleaveland and his settlers when he told them he was leaving (probably):

CLEVELAND HAS ITS OWN FLAG!

Wait, Cleveland has its own flag? Who knew? I did. I've actually owned two of these bad boys so far. And as a self-proclaimed Cleveland Ambassador, I have hung them with great pride outside each of the many West Side rental houses I have occupied over the years until I am inevitably evicted for varied and well-warranted reasons.

Unfortunately, my first Cleveland flag was stolen during the night in what can only be described as a heroic display of irony. So now I bring my flag in at dusk so that Cleveland can't steal my symbol of Cleveland. During the day, it flies at half mast to commemorate the loss of the first flag. And it will remain thus until flag #1's triumphant and safe return.

The Cleveland flag was designed in 1895 by high school student Susan Hepburn, which answers the question, "Why does our flag look like a teenage girl designed it?"

Let's break down the Cleveland flag design so that I can point out the various features and what I have decided that they represent. Though in full disclosure, I'll again admit that I have no research to support my assertions.

A. The three colors—red, white and blue—represent our city's renowned inability to think outside the box and its outright refusal to take chances.

B. I'm sure that the slogan "Progress and Prosperity" seemed like a good idea at the time, but now it seems like a sarcastic taunt from the past.

C. The year we opened this bitch up for business.

D. Christmas wreath meant to alienate non-Christians and warn them that neither they nor their heathen gods are welcome in our fair city.

E. Unidentifiable symbols that are probably supposed to look like actual things but just resemble plastic pieces from the game *Perfection* because some dumb teen girl from olden times drew them.

A BETTER CLEVELAND FLAG!

I think we can all agree that the Cleveland flag needs a serious upgrade. "The times, they are a-changin'," as Bob Seger so famously sang. And our flag should reflect the exciting new city that Cleveland has become since 1895 when everything was terrible and people did their laundry in rivers.

I have taken the liberty of designing a new flag that I believe is a huge upgrade. Mr. Mayor, if you're reading this, and I assume that you are, please consider making the following changes:

FLAG WITHIN A FLAG!

TASTY CORNED BEEF SANDWICH

BIKINI BABE (TOTAL 10!)

BOTTLE OF DORT

SWEET LAMBORGHINI

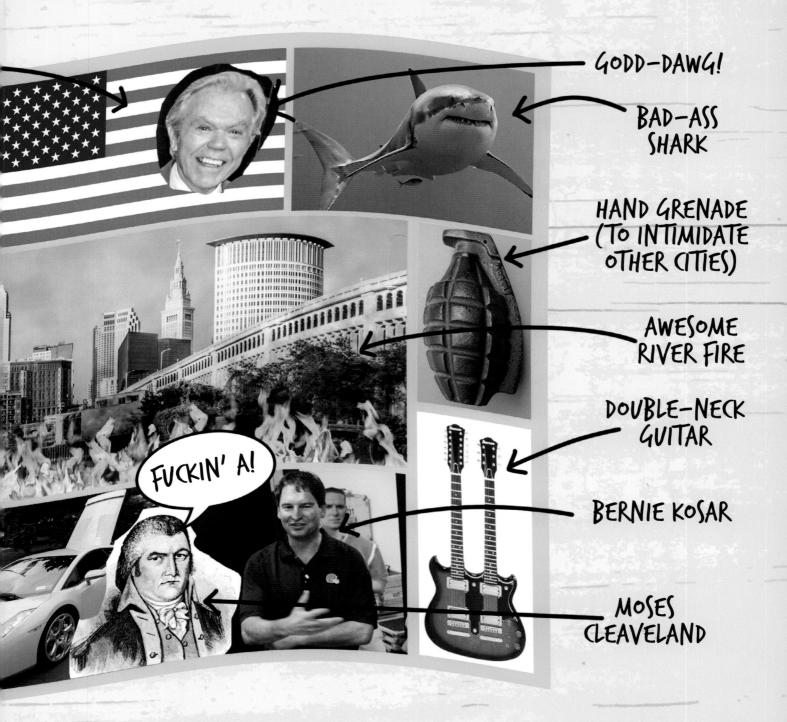

CLEVELAND'S
INDIGENOUS SPECIES

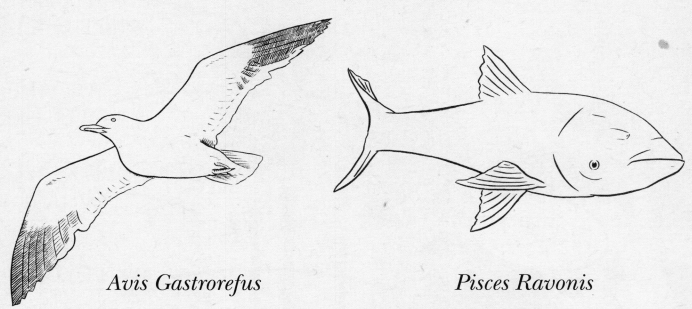

Avis Gastrorefus

Often called "The Rats of the Sky," seagulls heavily infest our city's lakefront and our suburbs' Big Lots parking lots. They feed on discarded french fries and styrofoam.

Pisces Ravonis

Often called "The Rats of the Sea," these merciless bottom feeders teem along Lake Erie's shores! Carp are infamous for their willingness to eat absolutely anything thrown toward them, whether it's a handful of nickels or a political enemy of a powerful Cleveland Teamster boss. No evidence!

OUR CITY HAS A VAST ARRAY OF NATIVE CREATURES! FOR ALL OF YOU NATURE ENTHUSIASTS, HERE'S A HELPFUL LIST OF OUR MOST FREQUENTLY-OBSERVED WILDLIFE.

Vermin Prolificus

Often called "The Carp of the Land," Cleveland rats have no difficulty finding suitable places to live due to our abundance of abandoned housing and impressive number of all-you-can-eat buffet-style restaurants with easily accessible dumpsters.

Currugat Boxus Domesticus

Often seen outside highly-attended downtown events such as sporting events and Rib Cook-Offs, these gentle scavengers add a vibrance to downtown that can only be described as "off-putting." They subsist primarily on monetary donations given to them by suburban visitors who succumb to feelings of charity or, more often, intimidation and white guilt.

HOW Bone CAN
Thugs A Harmony
HELP YOU AVOID DANGER

CLEVELAND is an exciting urban playground, and there's adventure around every corner! But not all adventure is good adventure. On more than one occasion, I have accidentally taken a wrong turn and ended up in a neighborhood that can only tactfully be described as "fucking terrifying." I have recently developed a little method that helps me avoid this potentially awkward scenario, and I'm happy to share it with you now.

It's pretty common knowledge that one of Cleveland's most celebrated rap groups is Bone Thugs N Harmony. Layzie Bone, Bizzy Bone and their fellow, similarly-bone-named comrades have produced several Cleveland-themed hits during the brief periods when they are not incarcerated.

The music is pretty solid, but the songs can also be considered a useful resource. I have personally found that it is in your best interest to avoid any street that Bone Thugs N Harmony have given a specific shout-out to in any of their songs. I'm by no means saying that something would definitely happen to you if you visited these areas; I'm just saying the likelihood is higher than if you were on, say, a street in Bay Village called "Barnswallow Drive." Just trust me on this one. Here is a list of streets that Bone Thugs shout out in their songs:

Shout Out Street: EAST 99TH
Song: "1st Of Tha Month"

Shout Out Street: EAST 95TH
Song: "Eternal"

Shout Out Street: ST. CLAIR
Song: "Da Introduction"

Shout Out Street: EAST 99TH (Again. Don't go there.)
Song: "Mo' Murda"

Shout Out Street: EAST 88TH, 95TH, 92ND, 96TH, AND HOUGH
Song: "Cleveland Is the City"

There. I've done my part.

WEST SIDE

Cleveland is dissected into two very distinct areas: the East Side and the West Side. There is, of course, a South Side as well, made up of such dazzling places as Brook Park, Parma, and Brunswick, but we find it's best to simply act like that isn't something that's happening. And if you took one quick drive through there, you would probably feel the same. So let's just concentrate on the East and West sides for now.

Personally, I am a West Sider. But I don't want you to think that this has somehow colored my perception of which side is "better." I pride myself on my ability to remain impartial.

We can argue all day about which of these areas is superior, and many people do. But the fact is, they both have wonderful attributes.

CHURCH

BOWLING ALLEY

BAR

WEST SIDE

vs. EAST SIDE

Each has great restaurants, historic buildings and unique neighborhoods. So let's just compare the two areas based upon street layouts. Below is a map that I have created from memory that illustrates the different approaches to civic planning that the West and East sides of Cleveland decided to take.

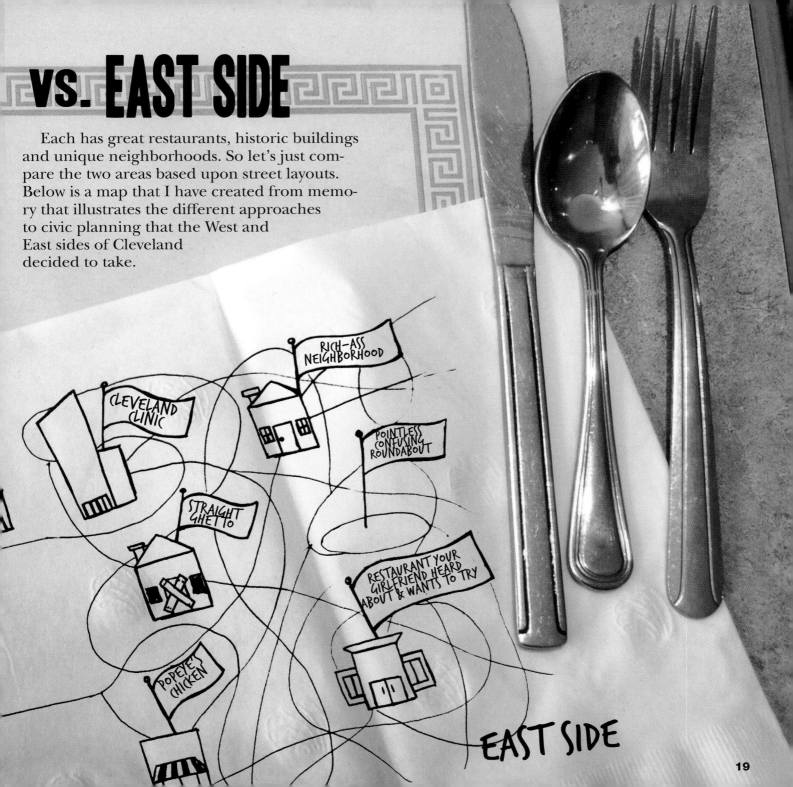

CLEVELAND CLINIC

RICH-ASS NEIGHBORHOOD

POINTLESS CONFUSING ROUNDABOUT

STRAIGHT GHETTO

RESTAURANT YOUR GIRLFRIEND HEARD ABOUT & WANTS TO TRY

POPEYES CHICKEN

EAST SIDE

CLEVELAND'S
FREE STAMP

SO THERE THAT THING IS...

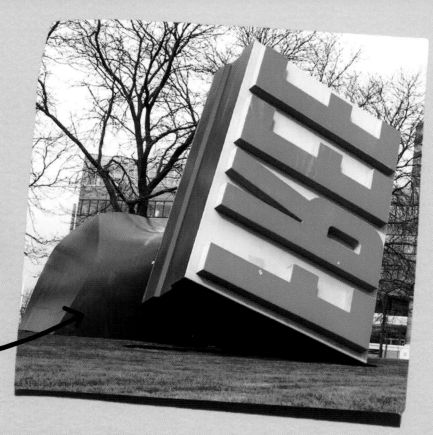

Hey, you guys, I was just thinking. You know what would be a better thing to occupy this prime piece of downtown property? Anything. Literally anything. Or, for that matter, nothing. Just grass.

The Free Stamp is one of those things that we have all just come to accept as part of our downtown landscape despite the fact that it's tacky as hell and symbolizes nothing. I actually did look up the history of the Free Stamp, and its story is even more boring and empty than its meaning.

It was made by some Danish artists in 1982 because Danes are always doing weird nonsense. Standard Oil had commissioned it to sit outside their new building downtown. They then were bought out by BP. BP hated it and didn't want it in front of their building because it's so stupid. They then magnanimously donated it to the city, in all likelihood because they didn't want to move it. The city put it in a warehouse for a long time because it was so stupid and ugly but then eventually decided to bring it out and display it, possibly on a dare. And there it has sat ever since, confusing and repulsing both denizens and visitors from around the world.

Here are four things that could replace the Free Stamp at this location that would both look better and be more useful:

GENTLEMEN'S CLUB

CINNABON

CLASSIC CENTIPEDE ARCADE GAME

FUN FERRIS WHEEL

21

(POTENTIAL) CLEVELAND BUMPER STICKERS!

Here are some sweet bumper stickers I made to celebrate Cleveland:

$ **CLEVELAND** $
IF YOU CAN'T AFFORD TO LIVE HERE,
YOU CAN'T AFFORD TO LIVE.

CLEVELAND
Now With *Slightly Less* Corruption!

PROGRESS & PROSPERITY

CLEVELAND:
LOSERS AT SPORTS
CHAMPIONS AT LIFE!

cleveland
pretty soon you don't even smell it any more!

CLEVELAND:
YOU COULD DO WORSE!

CLEVELAND

WE'RE JUST CRASHING IN CANADA'S BASEMENT 'TIL WE CAN GET OUR SHIT TOGETHER.

CLE VEL AND

TOO UNPOPULATED FOR A TERRORIST STRIKE!

REMEMBER THE FLATS?

CLEVELAND

CLEVELAND: WNBA-FREE SINCE 2003!

IF ANY OF YOU READERS WORK FOR A BUMPER STICKER COMPANY, YOU CAN HAVE THE RIGHTS TO ANY OF THESE IN EXCHANGE FOR A BOX OF T-BONE STEAKS. CALL ME!

MIKE POLK JR.'S THREE PLANS TO RESURRECT DOWNTOWN CLEVELAND

The Old Bait and Switch!

We have a casino now. And that's great. Because I've been saying for quite some time that what we really need downtown is a place for our citizens to unload all of this burdensome disposable income we're all so bogged down with. Maybe the casino will revive downtown on weekends and make it more like the bustling hub we've all dreamed it would become and less like the abandoned city in the movie *I Am Legend* (starring The Fresh Prince). But just in case the casino plan doesn't work, I have carefully developed three alternative plans to reinvigorate downtown that our civic leaders are welcome to implement as soon as I receive my $200,000 "consultant" fee.

Starting about fifty miles out, we change all of the signs that lead into Cleveland so that instead they suggest people are getting close to Chicago. Everyone loves Chicago! A lot of my friends have moved there. So, say you're some college kids who are trying to flee your backwater town to head for a new life in the Windy City. Or perhaps you're a witless tourist looking to spend some of your travel dollars visiting America's Second City. You set off on your journey and suddenly see signs that tell you you're much closer than you originally believed. Who knew that Chicago was only 25 minutes from Medina!? Once they're here, we just have to hope that they find our trickery to be amusing and decide to reward us by staying on for a while. The one caveat of this plan is that it will require citizens to wear Cubs jerseys at all times in order to help keep the ruse alive.

Giant Paintball Course

Don't worry, 30 business people who still work downtown, it's just on weekends. We won't ruin your Men's Warehouse suits. (BOGO!) Surely paintball enthusiasts would jump at the opportunity to compete in this sprawling urban environment. Plenty of condemned buildings to hide behind and homeless vagrants to use as human shields. It's a win-win! Admission: $35.

Operation: Increase Rich Arab Heart Surgery

It's no secret that the Cleveland Clinic is one of the best hospitals in the world. I don't know how it ended up here either, but it did. And people come from all over the globe to receive world class care. It's like knowing about a really good BBQ place that's deep in the ghetto. The killer baby backs are worth the risk. You've probably heard about the many Middle Eastern princes and kings who have come here for heart surgery. They pay top dollar to get their tickers fixed, pumping much needed oil and blood diamond money into our local economy. The problem is that we keep having to wait for the rich Saudis' hearts to go bad before we are able to get our mitts on some of their loot. The solution: We send several undercover Cleveland agents to work as servants in each and every royal palace in the Middle East. Once there, they get assigned to kitchen duty, and start heavily salting all of the food, consequently, revitalizing downtown. Don't look at me like that, asshole! It could work! At least I'm trying!

HIGHER LEARNING OPPORTUNITIES!

CLEVELAND HAS A VARIETY OF FINE SCHOOLS AT WHICH YOU CAN EDUCATE YOURSELF ENOUGH TO LEARN THAT AMERICA CURRENTLY HAS NO JOBS FOR COLLEGE GRADUATES. BUT COLLEGE IS A GREAT WAY TO KILL TIME IN BETWEEN HIGH SCHOOL AND YOUR INEVITABLE LIFELONG JOB AT A 24-HOUR FEDEX. HERE IS A QUICK BREAKDOWN OF FOUR OF THE AREA'S MOST NOTABLE AND PRESTIGIOUS ACADEMIC INSTITUTIONS:

CLEVELAND STATE UNIVERSITY

TYPE OF SCHOOL State college. You can get a college experience with the excitement of seeing people you thought you'd escape after high school!

CAMPUS "The City Is Our Campus!" is CSU's slogan. "And our campus is full of beggars and sirens!" was the rejected subtitle.

AVERAGE STUDENT Any young people who are riding the RTA. People getting their masters degree who are anxious to tell you that they went somewhere better for their undergrad.

PARTIES Let's just say that things get pretty nuts in their three dormitories, one of which is specifically geared toward married couples.

DRINK OF CHOICE Beer. Luckily, there is no shortage of vagrants willing to purchase beer for underage students in exchange for cigarettes.

LIFE AFTER SCHOOL Mid-level desk job. Unappealing family. Quiet, unremarkable death.

CASE WESTERN UNIVERSITY

TYPE OF SCHOOL Liberal Arts studies university. You can get a degree in really College-degree-sounding subjects like "Biochemistry" or "Philosophy." Guess which one of those two will result in a high-paying job!

CAMPUS Case owns most of the big, pretty, old-timey buildings in University Circle. They look like tiny castles in a kingdom full of Asians with backpacks.

AVERAGE STUDENT Slender. Foreign. Better than you.

PARTIES Mellow. Harmless. Most of the students attend parties so they can list it under "social skills" on their law school resumes.

DRINK OF CHOICE Keg of something not quite college-y enough, like Magic Hat. They're trying.

LIFE AFTER SCHOOL Mid-to-high–level position in another city.

CLEVELAND INSTITUTE OF ART

TYPE OF SCHOOL Art school. Worry your parents *and* come to class high? You got it, Picasso!

CAMPUS Two buildings: one looks like an abandoned high school; the other like an abandoned lamp factory. The Arts!

AVERAGE STUDENT Complicated. Insufferable. Thoroughly unemployable.

PARTIES Good music. Bad dancing. WARNING: Before the party starts, you may have to sit through a two-hour performance piece where a girl throws mutilated dolls into a yarn vagina.

DRINK OF CHOICE Discount absinthe.

LIFE AFTER SCHOOL Barista.

TRI-C

TYPE OF SCHOOL It's like an online school you have to go to!

CAMPUS Everyone commutes to a big brown building in Parma or a big gray building in Cleveland; you get to choose! You also get a locker.

AVERAGE STUDENT Prisoners taking classes online from Mansfield. Pregnant ladies who have a child at home who is also pregnant.

PARTIES Baby showers.

DRINK OF CHOICE Whatever you can sneak into class.

LIFE AFTER SCHOOL No.

VISIT THE ROCK AND ROLL HALL OF FAME!

HURRY, BEFORE THEY LET BON JOVI IN!

Cleveland Rocks!

Unless you turn on our local radio stations (mostly Ke$ha and Foreigner) or look at the upcoming House of Blues concert calendar (mostly Pink Floyd cover bands).

But as we all know, Cleveland is the birthplace of Rock and Roll. Not because the music developed here. That was in Memphis. And not because the roots of the music are from this area. That was mostly slavery-inspired southern blues that white people stole from blacks and then watered down for a caucasian audience.

No, we're the birthplace of Rock and Roll because a Cleveland D.J. said the phrase "Rock 'N' Roll" on the radio out loud before getting busted for accepting bribes during the Payola scandal.

We did it!

So now we're the home of the Rock and Roll Hall of Fame! An impressive structure that looks like the headquarters of an evil corporation from a 1991 sci-fi movie that's set in futuristic 2004.

Rock and Roll luminaries now throw us a bone and descend on our fair city once every three years to be inducted into the Hall. Which is somehow more insulting than if they never came here at all.

And, oh, the treasures that lie within! It's really impressive from what I've been told. I've never had the money to go in there. You see, while the cost of admission isn't overly prohibitive by most cities' standards, the ticket cost represents about half of an average Clevelander's monthly income. Which leaves many of us out in the cold.

That's why I have taken the initiative and started my own, wholly unsanctioned but far more affordable Rock Hall in the living room of my West Side rental home. I call it "Rock and Roll Hall of Fame 2*." Admittedly, our exhibits aren't quite as impressive as the "real" Rock Hall's, but admission is a far more reasonable two dollars, and you don't have to pay to park downtown because you can just park in my driveway. Just make sure that you don't park behind my upstairs neighbor Pam's Corsica because she gets pissed when she has to get to work and someone has her blocked in.

What follows are some of the awesome exhibits you get to check out, should you choose to visit Rock Hall 2.

*Apparently, I'm legally obligated to inform readers that my use of this name is currently involved in litigation and will most likely have to be changed. But as of the date of publication, the case is still tangled up in a lower appellate court so its usage is fair game! Suck it, Rock Hall 1!

"ROCK HALL 2"

Original Handwritten
Lyrics to Crazy Town's
Butterfly

Some of
Courtney Love's
Empty Pill Bottles

The Actual
Eddie Money
(Won't Leave)

Suicide Note from
Violinist Who Played
on The Verve's
Bittersweet Symphony

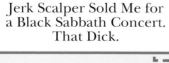

Fake Tickets Some
Jerk Scalper Sold Me for
a Black Sabbath Concert.
That Dick.

Red Hot Chili Peppers'
Back-Up Dong Sock
(Unused)

Chuck Berry's
Bathroom
Surveillance Tapes

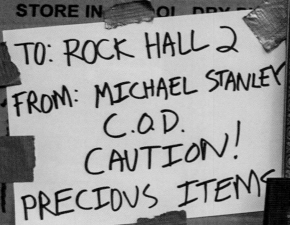

STORE IN ▮▮▮▮▮ DRY ▮▮▮

TO: ROCK HALL 2
FROM: MICHAEL STANLEY
C.O.D.
CAUTION!
PRECIOUS ITEMS

Michael Stanley

MSB
MICHAEL STANLEY BAND
AMERICAN TOUR 1980

Condom Found
Gathering Of
Juggalos 2008

Fred Durst's
Wigger Hat

Mr. Stanley,

Thank you for the unsolicited submission of your Michael Stanley Band memorabilia that you wish for us to display at Rock Hall 2.

Unfortunately, as has been the case the past five times that this box of your stuff has arrived on my porch, postage due, we are currently unable to showcase your collection.

Space is limited, as we have recently acquired the hat that Limp Bizkit frontman Fred Durst wore during his performance at "Woodstock 2." Needless to say, this display takes precedence.

Please do not take offense to this decision. We at Rock Hall 2 are certain that The Michael Stanley Band was indeed, to borrow a phrase from the letter you included, "The Bitchingest Band from Berea to Bay Village during the late 1980s." But unfortunately, we currently just don't have the space required to accommodate your signed albums, souvenir t-shirts and crude pencil drawings that you did of yourself. (Incidentally, the nudes were both unnecessary and needlessly graphic.)

Thanks again for your interest in Rock Hall 2. As has become customary, we have placed your box of collectibles on the front curb for you to procure at your leisure.

Respectfully,

Mike Polk Jr.
President: Rock Hall 2

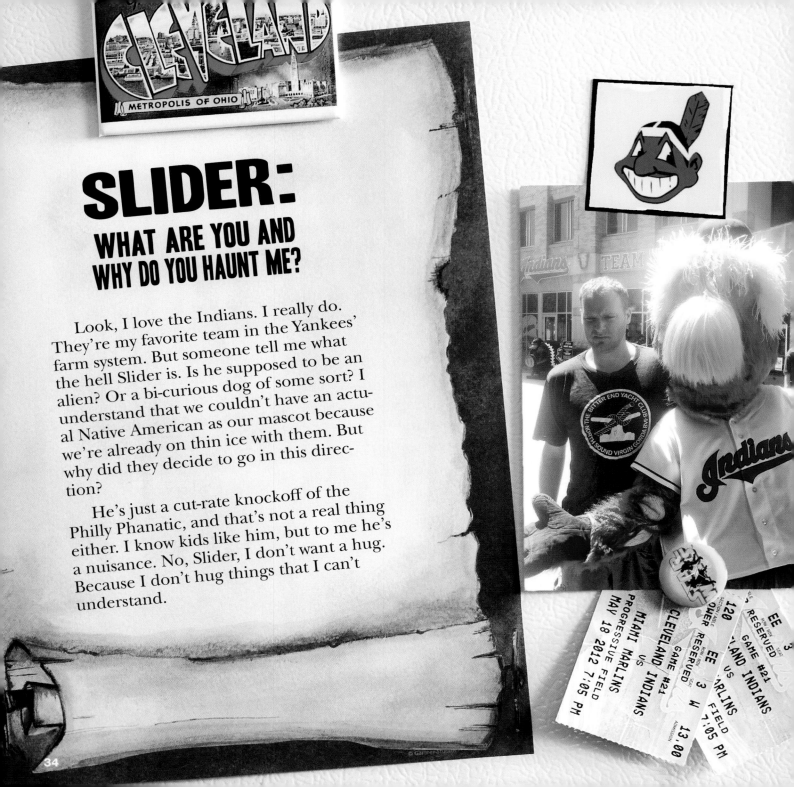

SLIDER:

WHAT ARE YOU AND WHY DO YOU HAUNT ME?

Look, I love the Indians. I really do. They're my favorite team in the Yankees' farm system. But someone tell me what the hell Slider is. Is he supposed to be an alien? Or a bi-curious dog of some sort? I understand that we couldn't have an actual Native American as our mascot because we're already on thin ice with them. But why did they decide to go in this direction?

He's just a cut-rate knockoff of the Philly Phanatic, and that's not a real thing either. I know kids like him, but to me he's a nuisance. No, Slider, I don't want a hug. Because I don't hug things that I can't understand.

TERRIBLE EVENTS IN CLEVELAND SPORTS HISTORY
(ABRIDGED IN THE INTEREST OF SPACE)

Asking me to pick a favorite terrible Cleveland sports moment is like asking an Irish Catholic parent to choose a favorite child. They're each special in their own way, and there are way too many to choose from.

So I thought it would just be best to focus on what are probably the four most notorious incidents in our city's long, tragic sports legacy.

I wanted to include actual pictures of each of these historic moments, but it turns out that it would be quite expensive to license the photographs and I'm only being paid $60 to make this book.

Though in fairness, the publisher also gave me this pretty cool promotional bookmark that I assume is mine to keep because they haven't asked for it back yet.

Anyway, given my meager budget, I was forced to recreate these events by employing the unpaid services of some of my listless friends. Though this admittedly isn't as good as having the actual pictures, I believe we did a pretty solid job of capturing these moments in a remark-ably accurate manner.

SCORE!

THE SHOT
MAY 7, 1989

Hey, everyone! Remember this!? Fun fact: I was actually at this game and witnessed the shot firsthand, despite being just 11 years old. It's a subject that seems to come up frequently during the now bi-weekly sessions with my therapist, Dr. Sanborn.

In case you are unfamiliar with "The Shot," or have relegated it to a dark corner of your mind as I had for a while using the timeless art of repression, it refers to Michael Jordan's game-winning buzzer-beater over Craig Ehlo that eliminated the Cavs from the playoffs. In retrospect, with all due respect to Craig Ehlo, maybe we should have had someone a little less slow and white guard the greatest player in NBA history. Or perhaps a double-team was in order. But hindsight's 20/20, as they say. LOL!

MICHAEL JORDAN (PORTRAYED BY MY ONLY BLACK FRIEND, BRIAN MITCHELL) RISES UP AND SHOOTS OVER THE OUTSTRETCHED HAND OF CRAIG EHLO (PLAYED BY A SMALL, HAPLESS CHILD)

THE DRIVE
JANUARY 11, 1987

"The Drive" refers to horse-faced Denver Broncos quarterback John Elway's 98-yard march down the field during the AFC Championship game that forced an overtime in which Denver won with a field goal.

Although I was a bit too young to be in attendance at this game, my father, a longtime season ticket holder, was there. Notorious for his small bladder, my dad was actually in the bathroom during the entire drive. In retrospect, this was undoubtedly a mercifully divine gesture from our benevolent Lord above.

JOHN ELWAY IS PORTRAYED BY FRIEND CHRIS CLEM WEARING FALSE, COMICALLY-LARGE BUCK TEETH. I'M FORCED TO MAKE THIS JUVENILE AND BITTER DIG AT MR. ELWAY'S PERSONAL APPEARANCE, AS I CAN NOT DENY HIS IMMENSE TALENT AND IMPRESSIVE NFL CAREER.

THE FUMBLE
JANUARY 17, 1988

Browns running back Earnest Byner fumbles the ball while just a few feet away from a game-tying touchdown, preventing Cleveland from reaching the Super Bowl and causing thousands of intoxicated Northeast Ohio men who were wearing rubber dog noses to cry for the first time since they were toddlers.

But as bad as this play was for the fans, just keep in mind that it undoubtedly led to a lifetime of total strangers approaching Earnest Byner at shopping centers and cautioning him not to drop the bag of groceries that he was carrying before cursing him under their breath and walking swiftly away. So it could be worse.

ERNEST BYNER (AGAIN PORTRAYED BY O.B.F. BRIAN MITCHELL) WATCHES HELPLESSLY AS OUR CITY'S HOPE AND PRIDE TUMBLE TO THE GROUND.

HISTORICALLY ACCURATE.

10 CENT BEER NIGHT RIOT
JUNE 4, 1974

This tragic sports memory was created not by any one Cleveland athlete or team but by the fans themselves. And that's what makes it so special. Though in fairness, the Indians' front office should bear most of the blame for this debacle.

In an effort to increase ticket sales, the Tribe held a promotion that allowed fans to buy as many beers as they cared to drink for just 10 cents each.

Who could possibly have foreseen that this would end poorly? And yet it did. By the 7th inning, it had pretty much turned into *Mad Max Beyond Thunderdome* with people brawling, charging the field, streaking, and throwing anything that wasn't bolted down onto the diamond.

Eventually, in the interest of safety, the umps decided to end the game early and awarded the victory to the Texas Rangers. Which was probably the first example of a game being called not due to inclement weather but on account of assholes.

If there is a silver lining to be found in all of this, it's that the riot compelled the Indians' marketing team to prudently cancel other potentially hazardous promotions scheduled for that year including "Free Chinese Throwing Star Night" and "Bring Your Newborn Baby and/or Pit Bull to the Park Day."

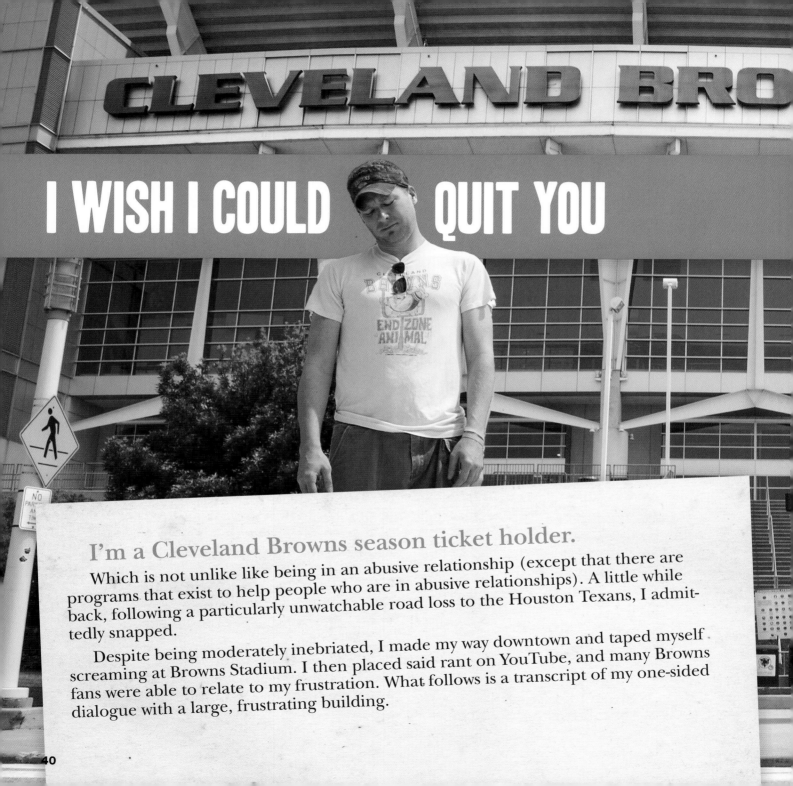

I WISH I COULD QUIT YOU

I'm a Cleveland Browns season ticket holder.

Which is not unlike like being in an abusive relationship (except that there are programs that exist to help people who are in abusive relationships). A little while back, following a particularly unwatchable road loss to the Houston Texans, I admittedly snapped.

Despite being moderately inebriated, I made my way downtown and taped myself screaming at Browns Stadium. I then placed said rant on YouTube, and many Browns fans were able to relate to my frustration. What follows is a transcript of my one-sided dialogue with a large, frustrating building.

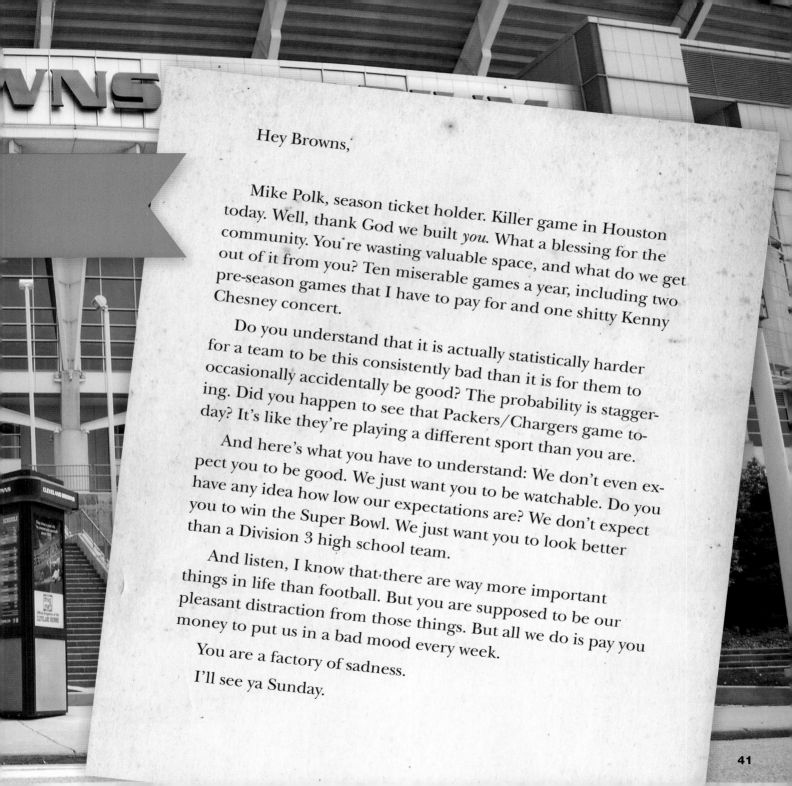

Hey Browns,

Mike Polk, season ticket holder. Killer game in Houston today. Well, thank God we built *you*. What a blessing for the community. You're wasting valuable space, and what do we get out of it from you? Ten miserable games a year, including two pre-season games that I have to pay for and one shitty Kenny Chesney concert.

Do you understand that it is actually statistically harder for a team to be this consistently bad than it is for them to occasionally accidentally be good? The probability is staggering. Did you happen to see that Packers/Chargers game today? It's like they're playing a different sport than you are.

And here's what you have to understand: We don't even expect you to be good. We just want you to be watchable. Do you have any idea how low our expectations are? We don't expect you to win the Super Bowl. We just want you to look better than a Division 3 high school team.

And listen, I know that there are way more important things in life than football. But you are supposed to be our pleasant distraction from those things. But all we do is pay you money to put us in a bad mood every week.

You are a factory of sadness.

I'll see ya Sunday.

THE GREAT CLEVELAND BROWN MUSTARD DEBATE

Cleveland has the good fortune of being blessed with two different delicious and popular brands of brown mustard that have long been associated with our sports teams. In fact, one could easily argue that these mustards are the most satisfying thing about being a Cleveland sports fan. (LOL!)*

There is a rigorous debate among some Cleveland sports fans and mustard aficionados** regarding which mustard is superior, "Bertman's Ballpark Mustard" or "Stadium Mustard." Let's settle this debate once and for all by comparing the features of each mustard in order to determine which is the superior product.

COLOR: BROWN
TASTE: REAL GOOD
COST: INEXPENSIVE

COLOR: BROWN
TASTE: REAL GOOD
COST: INEXPENSIVE

Conclusion: They're both excellent mustards and it doesn't matter. At all. Anyone debating this has far too much time on his hands and I think you need to seriously reflect upon your life and what you prioritize because you're currently going down a dark and lonely road, my friend, and it won't end well. You're seriously passionate about mustard? Really? Jesus Christ. People are hurting out there. Do you even care? Mustard? Sad.

* Did you?
** Losers.

DRAW YOUR OWN LAKE ERIE MONSTER!

*Note to reader: This is the first of three admittedly low-impact and low-effort entries that I have included in this book in order to reach the bare-minimum number of pages that I am contractually obligated by the publisher to provide. Thank you for your understanding.

ONE THING THAT BOTHERS ME ABOUT THE 1989 MOVIE "MAJOR LEAGUE"

I long ago came to terms with the fact that my favorite moment in Cleveland sports history thus far is the end of the movie *Major League*. Is it sad that my chosen moment of glory is fictitious? Probably. But it's all I've got.

Major League is a solid film. It's funny and inspirational, and despite the fact that the whole gist behind it is that our teams are a bunch of losers, it still portrays Cleveland as being a city with a lot of heart (though most of it was shot in Milwaukee).

But it wasn't until recently that I realized something that I didn't notice the first time I saw the movie when I was a kid, or in every subsequent viewing since.

The final win isn't really that big of a deal. It's just the pennant. It's not The World Series. I guess that should have been obvious to me, since we're playing another American League team in the finale, but it wasn't for some reason. I think I was repressing the knowledge.

The crowd reacts like they've just won a championship, but in reality, this team hasn't even entered the playoffs yet. They could still get knocked off by Toronto in the first round. At best, they will advance and eventually end up having to face the Yankees again. And let's face it, in a seven-game series, they probably wouldn't stand a chance. They're not going to buy any of Jake Taylor's crafty veteran bunt tricks this time around. Cerrano, our cleanup hitter, has only hit one curve ball all year. And apparently we only have two pitchers. And one of them is at least 60 years old.

But the saddest part about the film (other than the shitty sequels) is that this was supposed to be a feel-good fantasy film. Nothing in it actually had to be believable. That's the cool thing about movies: you get to just make stuff up. But even in our fantasy movie Cleveland couldn't win a championship. We had to settle for a pennant. That might have been our one chance, and we blew it. I blame Corbin Bernsen.

This photo compliments of my neighbor Pat's garage sale.

STUFF THAT HAS HAPPENED SINCE

The year was 1964. Everything was still in black and white. Drunk doctors smoked unfiltered cigarettes while delivering babies, and everyone was totally cool with that. This was the last year that Cleveland won a major sports championship.

I, of course, have to qualify it by saying, "major sports championship," because whenever someone brings up this point, there is inevitably some smart-ass rube who points out that we have actually won a championship in indoor soccer since that time. As if that has any meaning whatsoever. We've probably also won a national potato sack race at some point, but who gives a shit?

We don't live in Argentina. Soccer in Ohio is a thing you drop your kids off at to make them someone else's problem for a couple of hours so that you can run around and get some shit done.

Our last championship was won by the Cleveland Browns. And note that I have to say "championship," and not "Super Bowl" because it was so long ago that THE SUPER BOWL DIDN'T EVEN FUCKING EXIST YET! (Sigh.)

 **Gasoline was 31 cents per gallon.**

 **Al Gore had not yet invented the Internet!.**

 **The world population was less than half of what it is today.**

THEN

 **Betty White was 43 years old.**

 **The original *Star Trek* had not yet debuted.**

 **The movie *The Sound of Music* had not yet been released.**

46

CLEVELAND WON A CHAMPIONSHIP

Another indication of just how long it's been since we won anything is that the team the Browns beat that year was the Baltimore Colts, A TEAM THAT DOESN'T EVEN FUCKING EXIST ANYMORE! (I'm sorry for yelling.)

In fact, it was so long ago that the Baltimore team that we beat that year has since won a Super Bowl (1971), then stopped existing entirely (1984), then stole our football team from us (1995), and then went on to win ANOTHER FUCKING SUPER BOWL (2001)!

All of that happened!

But I'm not bitter.

What I'm trying to say is, it's been a bit of a dry spell for us Cleveland sports fans. In fact, in order to try to give you some perspective of just how long it's been, here's a list of some stuff that has happened since we last tasted success:

Ronald Reagan had only been a Republican for 2 years.

Man had not yet landed on the moon.

 We've gone through 4 popes.

NOW

We have since had nine U.S. Presidents! (Eight legitimate.)

Only men were allowed to run in the Boston Marathon.

A HEARTFELT PLEA
TO BROWNS FANS WITH CHILDREN

I'm a Browns fan. I always have been. But as this disturbing photographic evidence from my youth reveals, I never really had a choice.

From day one, my parents indoctrinated me into this lifestyle. I was never given an option. I was merely a helpless pawn in their sick little game. I was young and impressionable and simply accepted the fate thrust upon me. And I have never looked back—until now.

I've been thinking: Was it really fair for my parents to raise me this way? Considering all of the heartache my fanhood has caused me, could it even be considered a mild form of child abuse? I believe so.

Who knows how my life would have turned out had they not tainted me at such a young age? Perhaps I would have become a fan of a less soul-crushing NFL franchise.

Or maybe I would have never become a fan of football at all. Maybe I would have taken to a less-infuriating sport like professional wrestling, where everything is scripted and it is therefore refreshingly easy to get behind a winner.

This could have spared me a lifetime of frustration and dejection and probably about $50,000 spent thus far on tickets, stadium beers and ever-changing quarterback jerseys.

It's too late for me now. What's done is done. But perhaps my sad circumstance can act as a cautionary tale to you parents out there, so that others might be saved from experiencing my tragic fate.

So I am begging you, Cleveland-area parents, please be merciful. Give your children options regarding their sports allegiances. Wait until they are old enough to make their own decisions before introducing them to Cleveland Browns football.

If someone had only done this for me, maybe I wouldn't be paying $1,100 a year for season tickets that routinely ruin my Sundays and break my heart again and again.

Unfortunately, there was no one to speak up for me when I was a child. So instead I must now say, as I have said so many times before and will continue to say for the rest of my life: Go Browns! Brown and Orange Forever! And may God have mercy on our souls!

Mike Polk Jr., Section 341

RICKY "WRONG WAY" DAVIS' PATHETIC TRIPLE-DOUBLE ATTEMPT
(MY FAVORITE CLEVELAND CAVALIERS MEMORY)

The year was 2003. Zydrunas Ilgauskas had not yet quite given up on having hair and the Cavaliers were a formidable force in the NBA, dominating opponents with their powerful Chris Mihm/Smush Parker one-two punch. Except the total opposite of that.

It was March 16 and though Cavs had technically been out of playoff contention since the third game of the season. Yet tens of fans still flocked to the Gund Arena to be a small part of this 17-65 storybook season. A record that would secure us drafting rights to talented dickbag and all-around despicable person LeBron James, thus beginning an entirely new and different era of frustration and futility.

I happened to be at this Cavs game and was sitting in the Arby's luxury suite because my friend was named "Arby's Manager of the Month" in Cleveland. This game was his reward. No lie. Which just proves yet again that I'm a goddamned baller with an impressive running crew.

With mere seconds remaining, the Cavs were actually up big on the Utah Jazz. My friend and I were pretty much the last two people in the building at this point. Even some of the players had gone home. Yet we remained because the suite was filled with free beer and pizza, and we had no intention of leaving there until everything was gone or we were forcibly removed by management.

That's when it happened. On one of the final plays of the game, the legendary Jumaine Jones inbounded the ball to my favorite player in Cavs history, Ricky Davis. Ricky was just one rebound shy of a triple double and about two I.Q. points high of being considered legally mentally retarded.

Aware of how close he was to achieving a rare feat, Ricky Davis dribbled down to the other team's basket and gently threw the ball off of the rim and then rebounded it, unopposed, in an attempt to give himself a triple double.

I was the only one in the building who knew what he was doing, with the exception of DeShawn Stevenson, who took offense to this ridiculously selfish act of deplorable sportsmanship, and promptly threw him to the ground like a bitch.

The rebound didn't count, and Ricky came up short that night on the stat sheet—but not in my heart, where he forever earned a special place for taking an already terrible season to a ridiculous new low.

I was laughing so hard that I could barely finish the chafing dish full of free chicken fingers I was eating. But I fought through it and completed the task at hand because that's the kind of scumbaggery that Ricky Davis would have demanded.

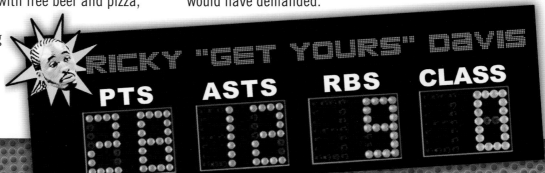

RICKY "GET YOURS" DAVIS

PTS	ASTS	RBS	CLASS
13	12	9	0

BECOME A PUBLISHED AUTHOR!

Here's your big chance to join literary greats such as myself, Ernest Hemingway, and Snooki by becoming a professional author!

Simply use the college-ruled area below to write your very own segment of this book! Be sure that the content is locally themed, snarky, and not spell-checked so that it fits the tone of the book. Good luck!

*Note to reader: This is the second of three admittedly low-impact and low-effort entries that I have included in this book in order to reach the bare-minimum number of pages that I am contractually obligated by the publisher to provide. Thank you for your understanding.

THE CHIEF WAHOO MASCOT
NATIVE AMERICANS NO LIKE 'UM!

Some people find the Cleveland Indians mascot, the lazily named "Chief Wahoo," to be offensive. A group of Native Americans holds a protest ("pissy pow-wow"?) outside the stadium every year on opening day to voice their discontent over the politically incorrect representation.

Now, I won't argue that the mascot isn't dated and comically offensive. But of all the things to be mad at the Indians for (re-signing an injury-ravaged Grady Sizemore again and again, letting two Cy Young winners leave in free agency within two years, astronomical stadium beer prices), this seems to me to be a minor issue.

"You don't understand, Mike, you insensitive, handsome prick! You're not a Native American!"

I suppose that's true. But I am extremely Irish. And the University of Notre Dame logo doesn't bother me in any way.

And they're called the "Fightin' Irish." They even put a derogatory adjective before their name that alludes to a common stereotype regarding the pugnacious nature of my people.

At least we didn't call our baseball team the "Gamblin' Indians."*

And just keep in mind that even though the current logo might seem insensitive by today's standards, it's not nearly as bad as the original mascot from 1915 seen below.

* Great point.

CLEVELAND DATING ON THE CHEAP!

SO YOU SAY YOU'RE IN CLEVELAND AND YOU WANT TO TAKE A HOTTIE OUT ON A DATE SO THAT YOU CAN TOTALLY TRY TO SECOND-BASE HER? NICE. GO GET THAT, BRO. THE PROBLEM IS, YOU DON'T HAVE ANY MONEY. DON'T SWEAT IT, MAN. CLEVELAND IS AN AMAZING PLACE TO BE BROKE. WE'RE SO GOOD AT IT IT'S NOT EVEN FUNNY. HERE ARE SOME SWEET FREE PLACES YOU CAN TAKE THAT PRETTY LITTLE DOE OF YOURS TO SWEEP HER OFF HER HOOVES.

FREE MONDAY AT THE ZOO!

THE GOOD NEWS: It's free!

THE BAD NEWS: Everyone knows this. The place is swarming with scads of disgusting kids that are all screaming that they want cotton candy and zebra rides. If you can deal with that, it's great. It's also a good reminder to pick up condoms next time you're at Walgreens. Lots of condoms.

EDGEWATER BEACH!

THE GOOD NEWS: It's free! And anything goes! It looks like there's a lifeguard there supervising things but it's actually just a scarecrow wearing a whistle that the city put in the chair to try to discourage knifings.

THE BAD NEWS: You'll probably get pink eye. And a lot of overflow sewage is pumped into here daily so you're pretty much swimming in stuff that came out of someone's butt yesterday, which isn't too awesome. But if you're date's not one of those high-maintenance broads, it's a good time!

TOWER CITY CINEMAS!

THE GOOD NEWS: This theater's legendarily lacka-daisical staff almost never checks to see if you have a ticket. So just walk in with confidence and enjoy!

THE BAD NEWS: If you go to see a horror movie there's a zero percent chance of you and your date hearing any of the dialogue over the constant sounds of people talking on their cell phones and instructing the actresses on screen not to go in there.

CLEVELAND AIRPORT HOLIDAY INN!

THE GOOD NEWS: There's always a wedding going on in here. Which obviously means free food and booze. Just place an elegantly wrapped empty box on the gift table and start celebrating "What's Her Face" and "Tuxedo Dude's" wonderful new life together.

THE BAD NEWS: Sometimes the bride and groom catch on to this trick. If you get approached and asked to leave, just keep your cool and handle the situation the way that I always do: Scream "A pox on both your houses!" really loudly. Then grab a chafing dish full of roast beef and make a dash for your used Hyundai that you left running, just in case.

Edgewater Beach BINGO

New Jersey
2, COOL
Garden State

4 Oz.
XXX

SUMMER JAMZ '94

So, you and your friends are visiting downtown Cleveland's picturesque Edgewater Beach Park—where the water is considered to be non-toxic enough to swim in upwards of seven days a year (if you are not pregnant, nursing or have a heart condition)! Congratulations! How about a fun game to pass the time? Be the first to see all of these indigenous Edgewater Beach sights and you win!

FULL DIAPER	BEARDED MAN SWIMMING IN CUT-OFF CARPENTER JEANS	UNATTENDED TODDLER WHO SEEMS VERY ACCUSTOMED TO BEING UNATTENDED
40 OZ. BOTTLE OF OLDE ENGLISH THAT SOMEONE CLEARLY CONSUMED THEN PISSED IN AND RESEALED	DOMESTIC DISPUTE BETWEEN TWO FAT PEOPLE THAT TURNS INTO A MAKE-OUT SESSION AND THEN BACK INTO A DOMESTIC DISPUTE	FERAL DOG FEROCIOUSLY PROTECTING A GARBAGE CAN FULL OF DISCARDED PICNIC LEFTOVERS
NEW JERSEY LICENSE PLATE (PERSONALIZED)	TWO KIDS WITH STICKS POKING AT A CONDOM THEY FOUND	BROKEN AND UNSPOOLED CASSETTE MIX TAPE LABELED: "SUMMER JAMZ '94"

MIKE POLK JR.'S FAVORITE CLEVELAND BARS

1219 MAIN AVE.
WEST SIDE OF THE FLATS

Anyone who knows me will tell you that I am a huge fan of The Nightlife here in Cleveland. The very fact that I capitalize "The Nightlife" should tell you just how seriously I take it. Cleveland has a vast array of really cool dance clubs, quaint upscale bars and trendy taverns to choose from. I do not go to any of these. Unless of course I am trying to impress a lady by pretending to be more urbane than I am. But if given my druthers, I prefer bars that are slightly more "rustic."

With that in mind, here are my four favorite Cleveland bars. I'm not saying that these are the best bars in Cleveland, I'm just saying that these are the best bars for *me*.

This is the oldest bar in Cleveland. It's now been open for over 100 years, but the bathrooms smell like it's been more like 200. This place has some miles on it, like a hot old MILF. And just like a hot old MILF, though it might not be the most superficially appealing establishment, it more than makes up for it with experience and technique. This place knows what it's doing.

Great vibe. Great bartenders. Great beer selection. And the perfect Cleveland bar vibe. Timeless and not trendy. Legitimately friendly but not a pushover. I've had many a great night begin and end here. My favorite memory was the night that my favorite Harbor bartender, Dan The Man With The Heavy Hand, was being particularly generous with the Jameson, causing me to wander upstairs (unbeknownst to him or myself), where I found an unoccupied couch and passed out. I woke up there at 5 a.m. and found myself locked in the bar. I didn't want to set off any alarms by trying to break out so I just went back to sleep and waited for them to reopen. I'm not relaying this tale with any great pride. I'm just trying to illustrate what a fine establishment it is.

FOOD & SPIRITS

1762 E 18TH ST.

1261 W. 58TH STREET

Becky's is an all-too-rare cool downtown bar. In a landscape dominated by shitty adjective/animal-named chain bars like "The Winking Lizard," awful dance clubs and trendy theme bars that will only be open for two years before becoming a different, stupid, trendy theme bar, it's nice to have a few real places representing the immediate downtown area.

It has decent bar food and good portions, a cool staff that cares and is happy you're there, spacious seating, live music, and an unpretentious clientele that I don't want to punch in their collective face.

It's also very close to the theater district so it's a good meet-up place before or after you pretend to appreciate culture. And it's right next to CSU, so it would be great for students who live on campus—if more than just eight timid foreign kids resided there. Check it out.

This joint is tucked in on the Shoreway and offers some cool views of the city. The neighborhood used to be shady but it has improved as of late due to hipsters encroaching and gentrifying it, because that's what they do.

I fell in love with this place because of their weekly Wednesday Blues Jam, the quality of which runs the gamut from "awesome" to "pretty rough" depending on who shows up to play. The crowd is surly and the regulars are mad that you're there. Which is endearing. They've got a killer jukebox and a useful patio where people blatantly smoke weed. (Unbeknownst to the proprietors, who are hereby absolved of any legal repercussions based on this parenthetical disclaimer.)

They also have good food and a surprisingly good brunch. That is, if you're not too highfalutin' to eat eggs that are served in a chaffing dish sitting on a bar bowling machine. Which, I assure you, I am not.

CORKY'S

I know. It's not a downtown bar. And I know that if I am going to cite this bar I should probably mention an equivalent East Side bar as well. But I don't live on the East Side. And I don't drink over there because it's too far to drunk-drive back, and I care about the safety of children who might be on the street while I'm driving home at 3 a.m.. Think of the children, people.

So even though it doesn't technically fit into the theme of this section, I am going to talk about my favorite bar in the Cleveland area. And if you don't like that, go write your own book. It's obviously not too hard. Look, I'm doing it.

The first time I ever went to Corky's there was no bartender working for some reason and there was a townie guy finger-banging a townie girl on the pool table. And it was the middle of the afternoon. No lie. I knew right then and there that I was home.

The crowd is typically pretty eclectic. It's a mix of bikers, ghetto, white trash, meth-heads, decent people, hipsters who are there ironically to laugh at everything and everyone and career criminals who are casing the joint to try to rob it later in the evening. And somehow it all just works.

They have karaoke here three to four nights a week, which most people would agree is two to three times too many. But once you become a regular to the extent that I have, you don't even hear it any more. It's like living right next to train tracks. It scares the shit out of you the first couple of nights that a train rolls through, but pretty soon it just becomes white noise. So now, when a fat couple whose evening will undoubtedly end in domestic violence gets up to sing Kid Rock and Sheryl Crow's wretched duet "Picture," I don't even notice anymore.

It's that kind of place.

There are between six and eight fights or near-fights at Corky's every night of varying intensity. I once saw a fight that ended with one guy getting stabbed in the leg with a pocket knife. The stabber then ran out the door for fear of reprisal. That's not the remarkable part of the story. The impressive thing is that the guy who got stabbed sat down and finished his draft beer before while waiting for his sister to come and pick him up. He didn't want to pay for an ambulance.

It's that kind of place.

Corky's drink prices are so cheap that the fact that they have a $10 minimum when opening a credit-card tab actually becomes a frequent issue among my friends. We will spend a couple of hours drinking and be ready to go our separate ways only to be informed that our tabs have not yet exceeded the minimum, forcing us each to get a round of shots in order to liberate ourselves from the establishment.

It's that kind of place. My kind of place. I hope to see you there.

A GUIDE TO
CLEVELAND GIRLS

LOOKING FOR LOVE IN THE BIG CITY? GOOD FOR YOU! HERE'S SOME ADVICE TO HELP YOU FIND THAT SPECIAL SOMEONE IN THE CLEVE. I HAVE BROKEN IT DOWN BY THE THREE MAIN ARCHETYPES OF CLEVELAND GIRLS THAT YOU WILL MOST FREQUENTLY ENCOUNTER. GOOD LUCK, CASANOVA!

DOWNTOWN GIRLS

BAR OF CHOICE

Anywhere that's horrible and has a roped-off V.I.P. section where no one remotely important hangs out. Usually one-name bars like "Sin" or "Air." The louder the better so that they can't hear their own conversations and realize how awful and pointless they are.

DRINK OF CHOICE

Whatever a douchey guy will buy for them. Preferably a $14 martini that's not really a martini but is a pretty color and has either chocolate or gummy bears in it.

MUSIC OF CHOICE

Anything with a beat that talks about dancing in the song itself and encourages ladies to "go for it."

ATTIRE

Full-on whore. Heels that become progressively more difficult to walk in as the night goes on. Dress or skirt that's nearly aligned with the vagina. More makeup than a rodeo clown.

SECRET TO THEIR HEARTS

Bottle service. Boat docked at Shooters. Or just a handful of loose paper currency.

TREMONT GIRLS

BAR OF CHOICE

Dark hipster bars with back patios on which to smoke hand-rolled cigarettes and loudly discuss books that they haven't even read.

DRINK OF CHOICE

Ironic Pabst Blue Ribbon or microbrews that are trying too hard with names that sound like gratuitous sex moves like "Rusty Elephant."

MUSIC OF CHOICE

You've never heard of the bands they like, and as soon as you do, they'll stop liking them.

ATTIRE

Meticulously chosen outfit that is supposed to look thrown together. Clothes are a combination of thrift store purchases and/or stuff that they bought at the store Anthropologie that look like thrift store clothes but cost them $800.

SECRET TO THEIR HEARTS

Telling them that the crappy music/paintings/photography/poetry that they create is amazing.

PARMA GIRLS

BAR OF CHOICE

Strip mall/plaza bars with names like "Slammers!" "Bonkers!" or "Jammerz!" that are usually located in between a laundromat and a Dots.

DRINK OF CHOICE

Jager shots. Whatever draft is on special. Mixed drink made in the ladies' room using the bottle of vodka they snuck in in their purse.

MUSIC OF CHOICE

Country songs about empowered women who don't need no man. Rap songs that were popular three years ago and are just reaching Parma now. Fucking Nickelback.

ATTIRE

Hairstyles that look like they're from a 1994 yearbook photo. Free t-shirts that were launched at them from a t-shirt cannon while they were attending WWE Smackdown at the Q.

SECRET TO THEIR HEARTS

Barbed-wire bicep tattoos. A steady landscaping job. Providing an adult male figure for her various children whose real dads have long since left the state.

THREE GENTLEMEN'S CLUBS OF CLEVELAND

Perhaps you're in town for a business meeting and you want to look at some breasts that are not your wife's breasts. Or maybe you're just a local horndog who has yet to experience our area's many fine gentlemen's clubs. Regardless, Cleveland has several exceptional establishments to choose from. So many, in fact, that it was hard for me to pick just a few to review for this book. But I believe that any of these three will give you a real flavor for what the city has to offer. (Note: Be certain to call ahead before visiting to make sure that these businesses are still open at the time you read this and have not been closed as a result of the dancers offering sexual favors to undercover vice cops in exchange for some Percocet.)

LOCATION: 1180 Main Ave.

STRIPPER HOTNESS: Cleveland 10s!

CLEANLINESS: Unparalleled! You could tell that they must clean there almost every week.

COST: Pretty pricy. I couldn't afford a lap dance so I just sat really close to guys who were getting lap dances and hoped to get some inadvertent residual grinding.

Located on the side of the flats that doesn't look like an abandoned haunted carnival, Christie's Cabaret is the premier gentlemen's club in Cleveland, primarily because it's the only one that employs women who you might want to see naked.

As I approached this majestic building, the exterior color appeared to change from pink to purple before my very eyes! The result, no doubt, of some sort of sexy sorcery! Color me "intrigued"!

The large, mulleted doorman was wearing a tuxedo, adding to the elegance of the establishment and making me feel like I was at the Academy Awards of titties.

Once inside there were scads of the hottest strippers that I have seen in Cleveland. And that is no exaggeration! Many of the girls even looked hot enough to work at lower-tier strip bars in Indianapolis or St. Paul!

LOCATION: 3029 W. 117th St.

STRIPPER HOTNESS: 3s and 4s. You can tell that some of them were probably hot in 1986 and some of them were probably mildly attractive until the meth finally won.

CLEANLINESS: Sticky.

COST: Perfect for a perv on a budget!

Located on W117th Street right next to an all-you-can-eat Indian food buffet, the smell of these two neighboring businesses combined can only be described as "life-altering"!

The prices here are suspiciously reasonable and should probably have been a red flag. There was a $2 cover charge that seemed excessively low until I saw what I was paying for, at which time I considered asking for a dollar back.

The strippers look like a bunch of your mom's middle-aged lady friends and I can only assume that many of them were hired over the phone.

LOCATION: 4980 W 150th St. (under a bridge).

STRIPPER HOTNESS: Not applicable.

CLEANLINESS: Though a dog-sized rat took my drink order, the service was prompt and friendly.

COST: Monetary expense was negligible but the emotional toll was steep.

Full disclosure, my review of Fox's Den might not be totally accurate because I think that I've probably repressed a lot of what I saw there so that I'd be able to sleep at night and some day once again believe that beauty and innocence could exist in this world.

Speaking personally, the women here did not appeal to me, but then we all have our different "types" that we prefer. And if your type is "failed cloning experiment," this might be the perfect place for you.

I congratulated one of the more attractive strippers on the quickly approaching birth of her child, only to have her correct me and inform me that she wasn't pregnant. I actually preferred thinking that she was pregnant because at least then I could justify to myself that she was hired to appeal to a specific fetish.

While I was leaving, I'm pretty sure that one of the strippers mouthed the words "Help me" in my direction and I thought about following up on that but my friend and I were pretty hungry so we just went and got eggs at Eat'n Park instead. So overall the experience was a mixed bag.

GREAT LAKES BREWING COMPANY

A.K.A. THE MAIN REASON MANY OF US HAVEN'T MOVED YET

There are a lot of things that Clevelanders aren't very good at, like making small talk or maintaining a viable economy capable of effectively sustaining a population.

But boy do we know how to drink!

Luckily, we are blessed with a great resource to enable our excessive love of beer, right in the heart of downtown, the majestic Great Lakes Brewing Company.

Established by brothers Patrick and Daniel Conway in 1988, the GLBC is a shamefully important part of our culture, and that's fine by us. Their delicious and award-winning beers usually have locally themed names, like Burning River Pale Ale and Lake Erie Monster. My personal favorite is the seasonal Holy Moses, named after our city's reluctant founder (see page 8).

But there are so many more potential local beers that they have yet to create! Here are just a few suggestions:

GREAT LAKES
BREWING CO.

Public Square Pete's Malt Liquor
A Yellow, Urine - Inducing Watery Brew

Cleveland, Ohio

GREAT LAKES
BREWING CO.

Case Med Student India Pale Ale
A Non-Threatening Level-Headed Ale

Cleveland, Ohio

GREAT LAKES
BREWING CO.

White Flight Light
Watch This Whiteness Dissappear From Your Glass

Cleveland, Ohio

YES, VIRGINIA

THERE IS A GREAT LAKES CHRISTMAS ALE

Great Lakes Christmas Ale is the regionally famous seasonal beer the Brewing Company puts out during the months of November and December that makes everyone's lives okay for a little while. With a 7.5 alcohol content, it is both notoriously strong and notoriously delicious.

It's often difficult to get your hands on this brew due to high demand by people such as myself with terrible priorities. I once almost fist-fought a middle-aged lady at a Giant Eagle over the last remaining six pack and my Aunt Judy and I have barely spoken since.

I enjoy Christmas Ale so much that a friend and I made a song about it. Just click on this YouTube link in your book to check it out:

http://www.youtube.com/watch?v=8kwF-TvMi_Q

Pretty solid, right?

Amazingly, Great Lakes Christmas Ale has somehow found popularity despite not having a catchy marketing slogan. So imagine how much more beer they'll sell if they decide to adopt one of these

GREAT LAKES CHRISTMAS ALE PROMOTIONAL TAG-LINES

that I just brainstormed after drinking an old six pack of the stuff that I found in the back of my fridge!

All I ask in return for my heroic efforts is just one complimentary Christmas Ale beer truck. You're welcome in advance, GLBC!

GREAT LAKES CHRISTMAS ALE: CELEBRATE THE BIRTH OF CHRIST WITH THE DEATH OF YOUR LIVER!

GREAT LAKES CHRISTMAS ALE: IT'S LIKE SANTA CLAUS IS KICKING YOU SQUARE IN THE DICK!

GREAT LAKES CHRISTMAS ALE: BECAUSE WHO WANTS TO BE CONSCIOUS DURING WINTER IN CLEVELAND ANYWAYS?

GREAT LAKES CHRISTMAS ALE: IT'S LIKE MOONSHINE WITH NUTMEG IN IT!

GREAT LAKES CHRISTMAS ALE: WHAT THE FUCK DID YOU JUST SAY TO ME UNCLE STEVE?! NO, WHAT DID YOU SAY!? SAY IT AGAIN! BUT SAY IT TO MY FACE THIS TIME, UNCLE STEVE! NO, YOU'RE MAKING A SCENE!

MIKE POLK JR.'S
LOCAL CELEBRITY FRIENDS

It's no secret that I am a huge Cleveland celebrity. It says so right on my Wikipedia page that I update daily. In fact, because most of my fame comes from Internet videos, I like to refer to myself a "CeWebrity." LOL! You can call me that too when you see me. I mean, if you want to. It can be a thing that we do. What? You don't want to call me that? Well why not? Oh, because it's "totally gay-ballz" you say? Well that's a little harsh. There's a nicer way to tell me that you don't care for that term I came up with. Oh well. Let's just agree to disagree.

Regardless, as you can imagine, the life of a local celebrity is a non-stop roller coaster ride of crazy times, raucous parties, and A-list social engagements. Let me introduce you to a few of my favorite fellow local celeb pals who I like to get down with on the reg . . .

THE NORTON FURNITURE GUY

Mark from Norton Furniture became famous the old-fashioned way: By creeping everyone the fuck out with terrifying late-night TV commercials promoting his affordable downtown furniture store.

Before I met Mark in person, I thought that he might just be something that I created out of a booze-fueled fever dream. Surely a man this spectacular could not actually exist in this world. But when I visited his store, there he was, standing next to one of his infamous decorative statues, looking just as real and nearly as animated.

A grand friendship has since blossomed between Mark and myself and he remains one of my favorite celebrity friends to cruise the bars with, searching for female company. We like to work in tandem on our quest for ladies, often incorporating such approaches as the old "Good Cop/Horrifying-Raspy-Voiced-Cop" routine. It rarely fails.

DICK GODDARD

This man invented weather! Literally! (Ageist joke #1.) Dick Goddard is a Cleveland institution and should also probably be in one. But that's why we love him. A man who after all these years still manages to get as stoked as he does about both clouds *and* neutering dogs has earned our respect.

God-Dog and I have pulled our share of all-nighters following many a raucous Woollybear festival. And let me tell you, if I had to give a forecast regarding a night out with him, it would be a 95 percent chance of fun with a 100 percent chance of us getting seriously messed up.

Shout out to D.G., just in case you're reading the large-print edition of this book right now! You're the man! Drinks soon!

TIM MISNY

I'll be honest; when I first met Cleveland's most intense TV lawyer, I was a little bit intimidated. His ubiquitous ads make him seem . . . how can I put this delicately? Fucking terrifying. That's why it was really interesting to find out upon meeting him that even though he comes off as kind of scary in his commercials, underneath that gruff exterior is a man who is in actuality much scarier.

Tim Misny once slept with another man's wife and then sued the man for emotional distress because his wife "was a real yappy broad." He won.

Tim Misny once sued a groundhog that was eating things out of his vegetable garden—and he won the groundhog's hole.

Tim Misny once sued himself for being too handsome. The case is still tangled up in court because Tim Misny is also defending himself and he's doing an equally excellent job.

You get it. Tim's a rad guy. Here's a candid picture that someone took of us during one of our weekly Tuesday night Twister games.

THREE CUTE CLEVELAND BARTENDERS

WHERE THEY WORK, WHAT THEIR REGULAR SCHEDULES ARE AND WHAT TYPES OF CARS THEY DRIVE

So now you're saying to yourself, "Boy, that Mike Polk Jr. is really tapped into the bar scene. He's a swinging player! A real man about town!" At least I'd imagine that's what you're saying. And boy are you right! Here's another example of just how "in the know" I am about Cleveland's night life! I hope you gentlemen find this helpful.

(All of these photographs were taken by me without the knowledge of the bartenders. Sometimes I use a timer and a tripod to get the angles I desire.)

ALLISON HATTON
Panini's
840 Huron Rd.

REGULAR SHIFT SCHEDULE (BASED ON MY OBSERVATION): Thu: 6 p.m,–close; Sat: 4 p.m.–close; additional shifts picked up depending on downtown events.

CAR SHE DRIVES: 2010 Honda Accord (navy)

HER TURN-OFFS (BASED ON MY EXPERIENCE): Close-talking; assigning her what I consider to be cute and sexy nicknames; shows of aggression towards male patrons who I think are hitting on her.

HER TURN-ONS (BASED ON MY EXPERIENCE): Not having someone make constant, unwavering eye-contact with her.

HEATHER MARTIN
Goodfellas
2217 E. 9th St.

REGULAR SHIFT SCHEDULE: (as a bartender) Wed lunch shift: 11 a.m.–2:30 p.m.; Thu: 4 p.m.–close; Fri: 4 p.m.–close; (as a server) Sat: 4 p.m.–close

CAR SHE DRIVES: 2008 Toyota Yaris (silver)

HER TURN-OFFS (BASED ON MY EXPERIENCE): Guys who take their shirts off in the bar to show her that they've been working out; guys who start to cry when they feel like they're being ignored.

HER TURN-ONS (BASED ON MY EXPERIENCE): Being left alone; remembering to tip her after having sat at the bar for six straight hours.

ERIN WALLACE
Third Place
3314 Warren Rd.

REGULAR SHIFT SCHEDULE: Tue: 11:30 a.m.–4 p.m.; Wed: 11:30 a.m.–4 p.m.; Fri: 5:30 p.m.–close; Sun: 4 p.m.–close

CAR SHE DRIVES: 2002 Jeep Wrangler (hunter green, soft top)

HER TURN-OFFS (BASED ON MY EXPERIENCE): Guys who show her their karate moves even if they're really good at karate moves; guys who sneak a flask of whiskey into the bar because things are kind of tough right now.

HER TURN-ONS (BASED ON MY EXPERIENCE): Me being quiet; her jerk boyfriend who probably doesn't even appreciate her.

SLAM POETRY TIME!

In addition to being an unsuccessful stand-up comic, author and lover, I also dabble in slam poetry. That's the kind of poetry where you try to make your boring poems less boring by yelling the words at people and scaring them. Black guys rule at it. Anyways, here's a slam poetry poem I wrote about a West 6th Street girl that I saw the first night I ever went down there. And pretty much every night that I have ever been down there since. Picture me yelling it at a disinterested crowd in a locally owned non-chain coffee shop to get the full effect. Enjoy!

DRUNK GIRL SITTING ON THE CURB ON WEST 6TH STREET

Drunk Girl! Drunk Girl sitting on the curb on West 6th street! 2:17 a.m. Why do you cry?

Hair cast asunder. Mascara running into intricate designs, making you look not unlike Alice Cooper.

Vomit pooling at your feet betraying your secret. Revealing the Panini's sandwich you completed just moments ago. Inarguably a capicolla, egg and cheese with extra slaw. A rare unintentional act of regurgitation for you. Drunk Girl!

In your left hand you hold a purse, relatively similar to the one you brought to the Velvet Dog tonight. A purse that you won't realize is not yours until the following afternoon.

In your right hand, you hold your weapon, a cellular phone red hot from overuse. It quivers in exhaustion as you type one last atrociously spelled text message to Kevin, reminding him that he is a fucking asshole.

With that task accomplished, you try calling Becky one more time.

RING RING RING! You demand once again to Becky's voicemail message that it tell you where the fuck she is, and when she is picking you the fuck up!

And with that, your battery dies, Drunk Girl. Leaving you disconnected, alone in this urban wilderness.

At the mercy of the fates and the universe.

Neglected! Rejected! Cruelly disrespected! And then! . . .

Salvation.

Just when you thought all was lost, three men whom you do not know with gelled hair and tight shirts approach you. These men, named Brad, Chad and Brad, have observed the state that you are in and gallantly invite you back to their house for "after hours." Drunk Girl.

These chivalrous white knights in shining Jeep Wrangler gather you up and squire you to safety!

"Safety" being their shared loft apartment above The Map Room on West 9th Street, where they will undoubtedly, irrefutably and indubitably run the train on you, Drunk Girl.

Goodnight, Drunk Girl. Goodnight.

THOSE
CLEVELAND
TOURISM
VIDEOS

THAT YOUR COUSIN EMAILED YOU A LINK TO

So a few years ago I made a couple of shorts called the "Hastily Made Cleveland Tourism Videos" and I put them up on YouTube. Clevelanders dug them and passed them around. And apparently other people did as well because they each have around five million views now and since there are only about eight hundred people still living in Cleveland this would indicate that some outsiders must also have watched them.

I did not foresee these videos getting passed around to the extent that they were, as I honestly felt that they were kind of inside and just pretty janky in general. But I think that's part of the reason that people dug them. The abysmal production value was part of the charm. And I wish I could claim it was intentional.

Most of the people that bring them up to me seemed to enjoy them and I still have drunk guys at bars scream mangled lyrics from these videos at me every now and again.

But of course not everyone was thrilled. The actual Cleveland Tourism Board, which I did not know existed, was particularly peeved and held a contest asking people to submit positive Cleveland videos to rebut my negativity. The results were earnest and utterly unwatchable.

I have also received a number of talking-to's from Pro-Cleveland advocates who lecture me about civic pride, and I even scored a couple of death-threat emails out of the deal. As of this moment they have not yet been carried out, but if I am killed between now and when this goes to print I can't help but think that it would really help move some books.

I'm often called upon by people to defend those videos and I don't really try to. I wasn't making some social statement or calling for any sort of civic action. Nor did I have any malicious intent. I did not put enough time into them to have a message in mind.

I was just being an asshole. I was picking on Cleveland the same way that a brother picks on his brother. Whether others can see it or not, the genuine love that I have for the target justifies the taunting, at least in my mind. But I understand that not everyone feels that way.

I honestly had a reporter ask me why, if I loved Cleveland so much, I couldn't have mentioned a couple of positive things in the video in order to balance out the message. I told her I was concerned that stopping in the middle of one of the videos to crow about our award-winning orchestra or world-renowned heart and vascular institute could have potentially muddled the humor.

She didn't get it. So it goes.

What follows are the lyrics to both Cleveland Tourism Videos. Amazingly, looking at the words typed out, it appears that these videos are even dumber than I remember them being.

Enjoy!

HASTILY MADE CLEVELAND TOURISM VIDEO

Fun times in Cleveland today!

Cleveland!

Come on down to Cleveland Town everyone!

Come and look at both of our buildings!

Buy some food that's prepared near the street!

Who knows, you might even see this guy!

You should come on down to West 6th Street!

It's the perfect place if you're a douchebag!

Watch the poor people all wait for buses!

Who the fuck still uses a pay-phone?!

Here's the place where there used to be industry!

This train is carrying jobs out of Cleveland!

Cleveland leads the nation in drifters!

Here's a statue of Moses Cleaveland!

He's the guy who invented Cleveland!

Yeah!

HASTILY MADE CLEVELAND TOURISM VIDEO (SECOND ATTEMPT)

Fun times in Cleveland again!
Still Cleveland!
Come on down to Cleveland Town everyone!
Under construction since 1868!
See our river that catches on fire!
It's so polluted that all our fish have AIDS!
We see the sun almost three times a year!
This guy has at least two D.U.I.s!
The Flats look like a Scooby Doo ghost town!
Don't slow down in East Cleveland or you'll die!

Our economy's based on LeBron James!*
Buy a house for the price of a VCR!
Our main export is crippling depression!
We're so retarded that we think this is art!
It could be worse though at least we're not…
Detroit!
…
We're not Detroit!

*damn it.

THE 98.5 MIKE POLK JR. GUARANTEE!

Stop reading. Turn on Classic Rock 98.5 WNCX. I guarantee to you that one of the following six songs is playing right now, or I will refund your money on this book.*

1. RADAR LOVE – GOLDEN EARRING
2. WISH YOU WERE HERE – PINK FLOYD
3. MISSISSIPPI QUEEN – MOUNTAIN
4. WHIPPING POST – THE ALLMAN BROTHERS BAND
5. STAIRWAY TO HEAVEN – LED ZEPPELIN
6. TOM SAWYER – RUSH

98.5'S PRIMARY CONDUIT: A BOOM BOX IN YOUR DAD'S GARAGE

*not an actual guarantee, but I was probably right.

FOUR GREAT PLACES TO TAKE A DUMP WHILE DOWNTOWN

If you're anything like me (and you should be so lucky), you occasionally find yourself downtown with urgent "business" to attend to: pooping. This is natural. When you have a lust for life like we do, periodic imperatives of the digestive system brought about by overindulgence in food and spirits just come with the territory.

But where to relieve yourself of this burden without concern of legal consequence? It's not always as easy as it sounds. For whatever reason, many downtown business owners frown upon people using their facilities unless they are "paying customers," because everyone's always trying to screw you.

Obviously, if you weren't downtown, this would not be an issue. There are plenty of gas stations and McDonalds' that can accommodate you. And they deserve to be shat in. I have long considered McDonald's to be little more than a public restroom that smells like french fries. And I feel no guilt whatsoever using them as such. I purchase nothing and give the manager the finger on the way out, often screaming, "That's payback for the McRib!"

But when you're downtown, it's a stickier wicket. There aren't any traditional fast food restaurants to speak of. And though the one BP gas station located by the freeway entrance on 9th does remain open, it's so ghetto that it not only doesn't have a bathroom, I don't think anyone is even working there. Word on the street is it was taken over by three homeless guys and a murder of crows about four years ago.

So if you have to deuce, you're going to have to get a little bit creative. That's where my world of experience comes in!

CLEVELAND PUBLIC LIBRARY
(325 SUPERIOR AVENUE)

Public libraries are a vagrant's dream! A quiet air-conditioned place with a public restroom that I can hang out in all day so long as I keep pretending to read an old *Newsweek* and not fall asleep? Yes please! Like all libraries, they try to discourage people from destroying their bathrooms and intentionally don't put them right next to the front doors in hopes of deterring trouble. But once you find them, these bathrooms are clean, quiet and pleasant. Bonus: Tons of reading material!

HORSESHOE CASINO
(100 PUBLIC SQUARE)

These restrooms are still relatively new, and they are part of a Dan Gilbert enterprise, so you know they're classy and built to last! Thanks Mr. Gilbert! This location is especially important because it's open 24 hours and it's nice to know that there's somewhere downtown that can accommodate our needs at any given time. If approached by security and asked if you intend to gamble before using their restroom, simply inform them that the real gamble would be in not allowing you to relieve yourself immediately before something terrible happens that scares off the uppity high rollers.

OLD ARCADE
(SPANS BETWEEN EUCLID) AND SUPERIOR AVENUES)

Take a dump in a historic Cleveland landmark! This 19th-century-style architectural masterpiece crowned by a gorgeous skylight is the perfect place to relax and unload. The restrooms are located in the basement and though the plumbing and facilities are quite archaic, they still get the job done.

THIS PORT-A-JOHN
(E. 13TH AND PROVIDENCE)

Normally slow downtown Cleveland construction is cause for frustration. But in this case, I hope that they never complete whatever this project is. When I find myself in a pinch, I've been using the port-a-john at this construction site for the last two years and the city seems to be in no hurry to finish the job. It's safe to assume that nothing will have changed by the time this book is published. And that is fine by me. "Is it clean?" you might very well ask. And let me assure you, it is not. Additionally, on more than one occasion I have had to temporarily evict a crackhead in order to use it, but beggars can't be choosers.

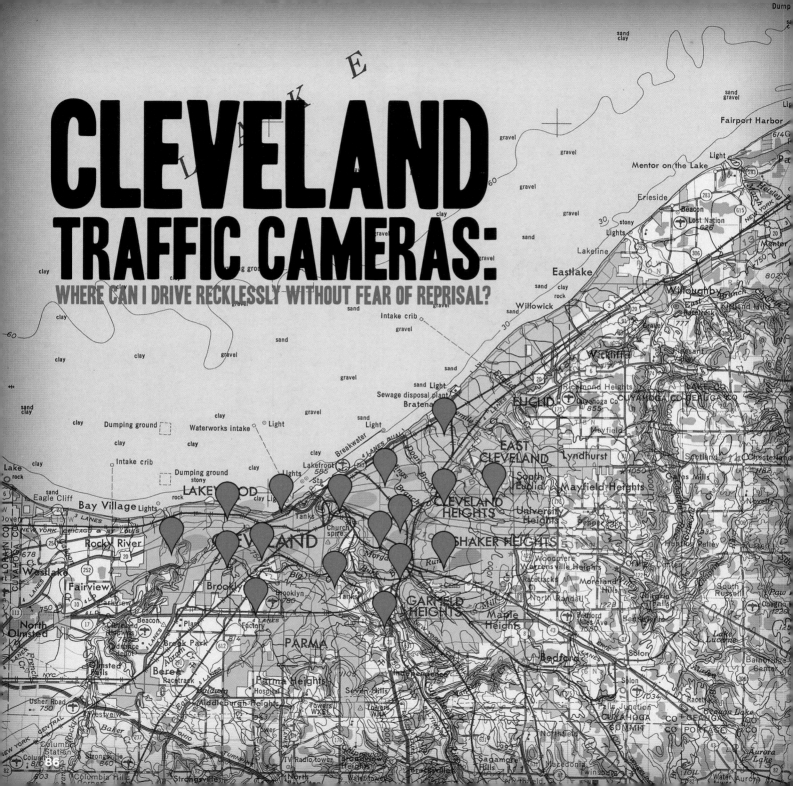

CLEVELAND
TRAFFIC CAMERAS:
WHERE CAN I DRIVE RECKLESSLY WITHOUT FEAR OF REPRISAL?

Not to hyperbolize, but red light cameras are the worst thing that ever happened to anyone in the history of all of time. And Cleveland is teeming with the bastards.

For those unfamiliar, a red light camera gauges your speed while you go through an intersection and automatically sends you a ticket in the mail if you roll through the light or go through too fast. They're hot little money makers and I've been busted far too many times. It's not even that I question their legality, it's just so impersonal. At least if I am pulled over by a human cop, I have a chance at talking my way out of the ticket. How am I supposed to offer these robot cameras 20 dollars or a quick HJ if they just let me go? It's very frustrating.

Each time I get a ticket in the mail, the "proof" that I did something illegal is a picture of my car sitting in the middle of an intersection. As if that proves to me that I was speeding. It's just my car sitting there! I can't tell how fast I was going! At least make the picture blurry so that it looks like I'm going fast, or Photoshop some flames coming out the back of my car to create the illusion!

The last time I received one of these tickets, I attempted to get revenge by writing out the check I owed them for 100 dollars, and then taking a picture of that check and sending them the picture in the mail.

They hated that joke! I went to jail for three weeks, which I considered excessive.

Regardless, in order to keep you loyal readers safe from "The Man," here is a useful list of all the intersections in Cleveland that have these pesky cameras. If an intersection is not on this list, you can feel free to drive through that area backwards while drinking a tall boy of Coors and honking your horn. Even if it's a school zone. Because I say so.

KEY

CHESTER AVE @ EUCLID AVE

CEDAR RD @ MURRAY HILL RD

EUCLID AVE @ MAYFIELD RD

CARNEGIE AVE @ E 100 ST

CARNEGIE AVE @ MLK JR DR

SHAKER BLVD @ SHAKER SQUARE

CHESTER AVE @ EUCLID AVE

WEST BLVD @ N MARGINAL RD

SHAKER BLVD @ E 116 ST

WEST BLVD @ I-90 RAMP

CHESTER AVE @ E 71 ST

E 55 ST @ CARNEGIE AVE

E 131 ST @ HARVARD AVE

CARNEGIE AVE @ E 30 ST

CEDAR AVE @ MURRAY HILL RD

GRAYTON RD @ I-480 RAMP

EUCLID AVE @ MAYFIELD RD

WARREN RD @ I-90 RAMP

PROSPECT AVE @ E 40 ST

E 116 ST @ UNION AVE

I-90 @ W 41 ST

I-90 @ W 44 ST

PEARL RD @ BIDDULPH RD

CARNEGIE AVE @ E 100 ST

CARNEGIE AVE @ MLK JR DR

MEMPHIS AVE @ FULTON RD

LAKE SHORE BLVD @ E 159 ST

ST CLAIR AVE @ LONDON RD

Rev. Michael George Polk Jr. 11/02

1320

12/17 '44

Pay to the Order of City of Cleveland $ 100.00

One Hundred smackers! Dollars

Have some of my money.

PNC
14205 Detroit
Lakewood, OH 44107

Treachery!

RTA PROTOCOL

Due to occasional situations such as a court-ordered-license-suspension-because-of-some-bullshit-that-wasn't-even-really-my-fault-but-the-judge-had-it-in-for-me-because-of-prejudice-probably, I sometimes have to find an alternative to driving my car around town. If both of Cleveland's taxi cabs are busy, this means having to use public transportation.

Prove that chivalry is not dead. Always be a gentleman and give up your seat to a man who is dressed as a lady.

If a gang fight breaks out on your bus in a dispute over drug territory, just keep reading your *Scene Magazine* and act like it's not happening. You don't need to be a part of that. Oh look, sexy personal ads!

2201

RTA

When you see someone urinating on the bus (and you will), don't scold them or turn them in to the bus driver. The bus driver doesn't care. Rather than cursing his darkness, light a candle. I bring an empty Gatorade bottle with me on every bus trip and I offer it to the vagrant when I see that he is clearly about to relieve himself. A little charity goes a long way.

When a crazy person stands up mid-ride and starts telling the whole bus that he is from the future and that our microwaves are going to rise up, unite and kill us all, remember to applaud when he is finished with his tirade. He worked hard on that.

If there is someone dead on the bus (and there will be), your initial reaction might be to alert the bus driver. Don't do this. The bus driver doesn't care. Just put a pair of sunglasses on him so that he does not frighten the children on the bus. For an added touch, manipulate his mouth so that it is frozen in a rigor mortised perma-smile. Hey kids, who's that happy cool dude in the back of the bus? Definitely not a dead guy. See? It worked.

LUCKY MAKE-A-WISH PAGE!

Concentrate really hard. Think about your deepest desire! Really visualize it! Now rub Mayor Frank Jackson's beard and make your wish! Now go throw this book into Lake Erie!** Your wish is guaranteed to come true!***

* Note to reader: This is the third of three admittedly low-impact and low-effort entries that I have included in this book in order to reach the bare-minimum number of pages that I am contractually-obligated by the publisher to provide. Thank you for your understanding.

** Replacement copies of this book are available at www.amazon.com or that first gross aisle at Marc's discount grocery stores throughout Greater Cleveland.

*** Not a real guarantee.

CLEVELAND ADVENTURE MAD LIBZ*!

Remember the classic, wacky, make-em-up, word game Mad Libz?! Well I thought it would be fun** to include a Cleveland-themed Mad Libz! You know how this works. Just grab a friend who likes to laugh and ask them to give you the following parts of speech! Then read it back to them and get ready for some hearty guffaws! Have fun!

It was another crazy weekend in _____ Cleveland, Ohio. Some friends and I decided to go to the
(NEGATIVE ADJECTIVE)

_____ concert at _____ We knew it was going to be a _____ night!
(ONCE POPULAR BAND)   (LOCAL CONCERT VENUE)   (POSITIVE ADJECTIVE)

And _____ knows we could all use it, because we were still in a really _____ mood after
(DEITY YOU WORSHIP)   (NEGATIVE ADJECTIVE)

watching the _____ game. Every time we think we've seen every possible way to lose, those
(ANY CLEVELAND SPORTS TEAM)

_____ _____ find a new way to disappoint us. Boy, they sure are _____.
(VULGAR ADJECTIVE) (SAME SPORTS TEAM)   (THE WORD "TERRIBLE")

_____ agreed to be the Designated Driver for the night, which was awesome because that allowed
(NAME OF YOUR LEAST POPULAR FRIEND)

the rest of us to get _____ in the car on
(TERM TO DESCRIBE EXTREME STATE OF DRUNKENNESS. I RECOMMEND "SHIT-TRAINED" BUT IT'S YOUR STORY)

the way there.

The show itself was really _____, that is until _____ Mike Polk Jr. showed up. As always, as soon
(NEGATIVE ADJECTIVE)   (POSITIVE ADJECTIVE)

as he got there the night became _____ Because as anyone will tell you, no one does stuff as
(EXTREMELY POSITIVE ADJECTIVE)

_____ as Mike. He's even cooler than _____.
(POSITIVE ADVERB)   (NAME OF THE COOLEST PERSON YOU KNOW BUT YOU CAN'T USE "MIKE POLK")

Mike drank _____ shots and then left the show with _____ attractive women. The hot girls all
(VERY HIGH NUMBER)   (EVEN HIGHER NUMBER)

went back to Mike's place and they didn't think it was _____ that he lived in the upstairs of a rental house even
(NEGATIVE ADJECTIVE)

though he was in his mid-thirties. In fact they thought it was _____. So much so that they let Mike do
(POSITIVE ADJECTIVE)

_____ and _____ and plus _____ to them all night long, again and again.
(TAWDRY SEX ACT)   (ANOTHER TAWDRY SEX ACT)   (BORDERLINE CRIMINAL SEX ACT)

The End.

That's it! Now read it out loud! Hilarious, right!? Now post the completed story on your Facebook page with no explanation. Now tag me! You did it!

* It turns out that "Mad Libs" is a trademarked term, which is why we decided to call our word game "Mad Libz" with a "z," thereby making it good and legal. Probably. Or maybe not. I don't know. What am I, a goddamned lawyer?

** Take up space.

CLEVELAND THRIFTING LIKE A PRO!

We have a motto in Cleveland. "Why pay full price for a new pair of bed sheets when you can buy a used set that some guy died in for so much less?"

Well, it's not really a motto yet. Not officially. But I've been trying to get it to catch on.

Thrift stores are a Cleveland way of life. With 96% of our population being well under the poverty line, they provide an invaluable and affordable way for us to keep passing around our used blue jeans to each other.

Whether you're an obnoxious hipster trying to find ironic things like Kenny Rogers' The Gambler records and t-shirts with American flags/wolves on them or you're a Latina mother of 16 trying desperately to shoe your niños, it's important to know that all Cleveland thrift stores are not created equal. With that in mind, here are my three personal favorite places to shop for cheap wares that smell like your grandma's house.

10694 LORAIN AVENUE

Nestled lovingly between a store where you can rent furniture by the week and a T.J. Maxx where the staff doesn't even pretend to try and keep the clothes off the floor, this near West Side establishment has great prices and a great selection. Warning: beggars flock like pigeons to this parking lot and you will be hit up at least five times on your way to and from your car, which may or may not be there when you come out. So stay frosty.

FEATURED ITEM THAT CAUGHT MY EYE:

There was no other ski in sight. It's just this one. Which is obviously not ideal. Unless the potential consumer already owns just one ski that is the same or at least very similar to this ski. Or is, perhaps, some sort of heroic amputee who refuses to give up on the dream. But regardless, very affordable at just $7.50.

4633 NORTHFIELD ROAD

This whole area is really the Shangri-La of Cleveland thrifting. This plaza alone contains three different thrift stores! And a Big Lots! And a Dollar General! It's sort of the opposite of nearby, ritzy Legacy Village. But I find the people here to be less revolting. The Salvation Army is my favorite of the triad in this budget plaza. Orderly shelves, good discount days, and a helpful and friendly staff who don't look at you judgmentally when you buy bath towels.

FEATURED ITEM THAT CAUGHT MY EYE:

Just because he hasn't played since 2003 and was terrible while he was here doesn't mean you shouldn't continue to support him by buying this "classic throwback" jersey for just two dollars. Bonus: Tim Couch now works here and will sign it for you!

3333 LORAIN AVENUE

There are several Uniques in town but this is the Mothership. It's primarily famous for it's "Half-Price Monday" special that brings out the best and brightest of Cleveland's thrifting consumers. This place has it all. Need an affordable, plus-size bridal gown in a hurry? This is your spot. Want a watercolor painting of a black Jesus in a frame made entirely of seashells? Unique has you covered. Bonus: If you get hungry from picking through people's garbage all day, there's a hot dog vendor in the parking lot who apparently doesn't comprehend how gross that is.

FEATURED ITEM THAT CAUGHT MY EYE:

I don't know why this naked baby doll is holding a VHS copy of *Weekend At Bernie's 2 (Bernie's Back, and He's Still Dead!)*, but it is. And I think that's terrific.

CLEVELAND ENEMY HALL OF FAME

Jimmy Dimora

This magnificent scumbag is the paragon of Cleveland goon politics that ruled the city for decades. He now resides at a federal correctional facility where he spends his nights crying and his days not even considering exercising.

Scut Farkus

The bully from the holiday classic *A Christmas Story* might not be a real person, but he was a mega-jerk. And the movie was shot in Cleveland. I'm actually just mad because I grew up looking exactly like this kid. Which wasn't a good thing.

Art Modell

You know what he did. And he has since shed his earthly coil. I am trying to start an initiative to have his remains moved to a different city every five years. But so far it's not catching on and one person called me "ghastly."

EVERY CITY HAS ENEMIES.
CHICAGO HAD AL CAPONE, GOTHAM HAD THE JOKER, LITTLE ROCK HAD CIVIL RIGHTS.
HERE ARE CLEVELAND'S MOST NOTORIOUS VILLAINS.

Asian Carp

These sneaky bastards are threatening to dominate our pristine waters and crowd out all of our precious walleye! Which wouldn't be so bad if they didn't taste like shit and look like Steve Buscemi!

LeBron James

The gracelessness of his exit is legendary. But say what you will, he obviously knew that he was not capable of winning a championship without at least two other All Stars. Now if only he were not too dumb to understand how meaningless that makes his ring.

Road Constru

Maybe if it didn't take s workers three months to pothole this wouldn't be hassle. How can rush h be so slow in a city wit jobs? Because every ot is constantly closed.

AHOY!
ALL ABOARD THE GRODIEST BOAT
ON THE SEVEN SEAS!
IT'S THE...

Cleveland Steamer!

HOW AND WHEN TO TELL YOUR KIDS ABOUT "THE CLEVELAND STEAMER"

They say that there's no such thing as bad publicity. And I guess having a depraved sex act named after our city is an honor in some strange way. But that doesn't mean it's not uncomfortable to talk about. Your children* are eventually bound to hear some classmates talking about The Cleveland Steamer on the playground. And it's better for you to give them the real facts about this natural milestone in every healthy relationship than for them to hear about it on the streets. So here, for your benefit, is a little speech you can give your kids when you decide it's time to have "the talk." You might want to cut this out and keep it in your wallet so you're good to go when the moment presents itself.

Son/Daughter, it's time we had a very important chat. You've probably heard some of your friends at school talking about *The Cleveland Steamer* and you might be a little confused. That is totally natural and nothing to be embarrassed about. You see Son/Daughter, when a mommy and daddy love each other very much, there comes a point in the relationship when they want to take it to "the next level." One way of expressing this love for each other is for the daddy to stand astride the mommy who is lying on her back, helplessly prone in nervous anticipation. Daddy then defecates on Mommy and rolls around in it like a steamroller. I can see that this is upsetting you. Now, I know it sounds unpleasant Son/Daughter, maybe even a little bit gross. But believe me when I say that one day you'll understand what it means to . . . wait, Son/Daughter, where are you going? Why are you crying? Come back here! This is my house and you will respect me! Unlock this door! (etc.)

*You have kids? Gross.

98

LESSER KNOWN NORTHERN-OHIO-THEMED SEX ACTS

The Cleveland Steamer is by far our most famous regionally-named sex act, but there are others. And I feel that they have been living in the shadow of the Steamer for far too long and deserve some acknowledgement. My gentlemanly nature forbids me from going into specific detail regarding what is involved in each of these moves, but I will now list five of them and use them in a conversational context in which they might appear.

I just had to throw out my favorite set of sheets cause I got drunk and gave some girl a **Willoughby Chili Dog**.

You know that chick who works at The Dollar Tree who's hot except she has a lazy eye? Dave and I totally gave her a **Parma Paddleboat.**

Then we high-fived.

Remember that bully Craig who went to our high school? I heard the cops caught him in a baseball dugout giving some other dude a **Lakewood Lollipop**.

I don't know what kind of a girl you think I am, but there's no way in hell I'm doing a **Brook Park Bus Stop**. So you can just tell all your friends to go home.

Everything was going pretty well, and then, without even warning me, she tried to give me a **Toledo Mudhen**. So I just went with it.

HAUNTED CLEVELAND LANDMARKS!

To be candid, I don't personally believe in ghosts. I tend to attribute this character flaw to the fact that I am not a teen girl or an idiot. But if you are a believer and that's you're thing, more power to you. And if you're looking for something spooky to do around the Cleveland area, you have plenty of options.

Obviously if it's around October there are a variety of seasonal "Haunted" attractions at various fairgrounds you can attend. They traditionally involve stoned, outcast teens wearing poorly-applied makeup who jump out at you while the piano theme from the movie *Halloween* plays and incessant strobe lights make you increasingly nauseous. This costs 25 dollars.

But if you're looking for the real deal, check out some of these super-legitimate Haunted Cleveland landmarks.

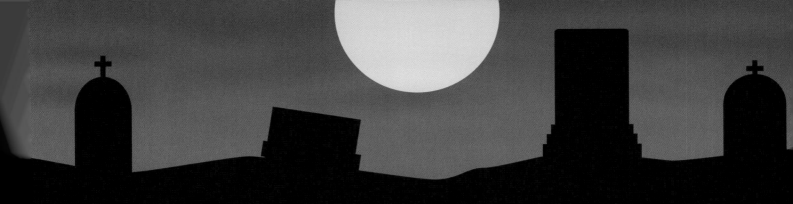

FRANKLIN CASTLE

This huge, Gothic stone mansion located in Ohio City is said to be haunted as the result of a great tragedy that occurred within it. And I'm not just talking about the heating bill! LOLOLOLOLOL!*

In the late 1800s, the castle was owned by a man named Hannes Tiedemann who, according to legend, (and by "legend," I obviously mean a website that I briefly looked at), lost his three children to illness. This caused the grieving Hannes, who was apparently the kind of person who blows everything way out of proportion, to subsequently murder his niece and a servant girl that also lived at the manor. (Speaking of "murder," how about the heating bill for this place? Am I right?**)

It is said that the restless and tortured spirits of these tragic victims now haunt the castle, which sucks for those ghosts but is terrific for tourism.

Someone recently tried to shoot a ghost-based reality show in the castle that never made it to the air. And in light of how many unspeakably terrible reality shows are currently airing, the fact that this one could not find a home, not even on SpikeTV, is just further proof that the building is truly cursed.

4308 Franklin Blvd

*I am a professional comedian. If you enjoy great jokes like that one, my stand up CD is available for purchase at www.mikepolkir.com

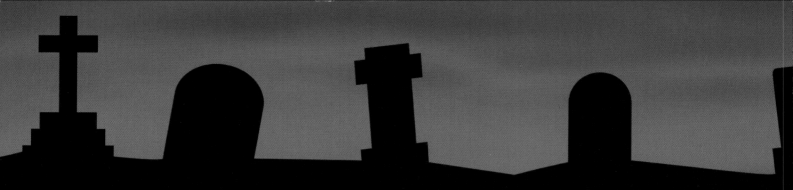

THE DRURY MANSION 8625 Euclid Ave.

This 52-room mansion was constructed in 1912 by Francis Drury. According to legend, this is where the house got it's name.

The place is rumored to be haunted by the ghost of a woman with long brown hair, dressed in clothing from the turn of the century, suggesting that even Cleveland's ghost-women are unable to stay on top of modern fashion.

The ominous building is full of twisting corridors that open into oddly placed rooms. There is even a secret tunnel on the lower floor that leads beneath Euclid Avenue to the old Cleveland Play House's Drury Theater. This convenient feature allows ghosts to sneak into local productions of *Joseph and The Amazing Technicolor Dreamcoat* without paying admission.

The Drury Mansion was recently purchased by the Cleveland Clinic. Haunted Tours are available for a 20 dollar co-pay if you are in the Clinic's insurance network. If not, admission is $18,000.

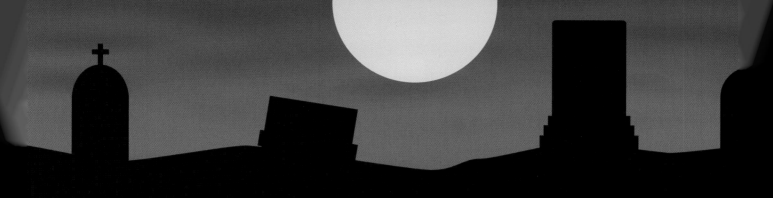

ERIE STREET CEMETERY Between E. 9th and E. 14th streets (right across from Progressive Field)

Cleveland's second oldest cemetery was founded in 1826 and contains the remains of over 17,000 Clevelanders, many of whom have somehow managed to continue voting for Democratic candidates well after their demise.

Erie Street Cemetery is rumored to be haunted by two Native Americans who are buried there: Joc-O-Sot and Chief Thunderwater. Thunderwater is said to be the model for the Cleveland Indians mascot, the universally cherished and not-at-all-culturally-offensive "Chief Wahoo."

Reported sightings of the two ghosts have all but ceased as of late, leading many to believe that the spirits have abandoned the cemetery because they were sick of downtown vagrants pestering them for spare ghost change.

CLEVELAND BROWNS STADIUM 100 Alfred Lerner Way

Abandon All Hope, Ye Who Enter Here! As soon as you pay your 75 dollars to walk into this eerie monstrosity, you are immediately overcome by the sensation that countless terrible tragedies have occurred here. (Trent Dilfer anyone?) Okay. This is too easy. I'm just going to walk away from this one. But you get it.

FOUR SWELL SPOTS AROUND CLEVELAND THAT MAKE ME TEMPORARILY FORGET HOW POINTLESS AND BLEAK MAN'S EXISTENCE IS

THIS PLACE IN LAKEWOOD PARK

Fight your way through the gauntlet of chubby, power-walking moms and obnoxious toddlers who are screaming for fresh juice boxes. Head for the lake. Walk down the endless staircase. (Are you drunk? Me too! Watch your step!) You'll be rewarded with a gorgeous view of the city. Close enough to feel connected but far enough away that your wallet is safe. Enjoy.

ROCKY RIVER METRO PARKS

A lot of people use this place to work out. And that's fine. If people want to waste their lives running and biking and kayaking like they're in a goddamned Code Red Mountain Dew commercial so that they can live two years longer than I will, have at it. I come here to walk around and hang out. Lots of really nice views, uncrowded walking paths and serene nature that is surprisingly close to the city. If you're looking for some vast woods to do some creepy stuff in, you could do worse.

WADE PARK LAGOON

This is a perfect little cultural oasis that contrasts intensely with our predominantly rusty city. Located right behind the Cleveland Museum of Art, which contains lots of awesome, old-timey, naked-lady oil paintings (va-va-voom!), this is a truly unique and lovely area in which to either sit and quietly contemplate your life or to try and photo-bomb some bride's carefully-orchestrated wedding pictures.

STONES LEVEE AREA IN THE FLATS

While probably not technically aesthetically pleasing, there is something very cool about this area and everybody should check it out. It's a reminder of the industry that the city was founded upon and though a lot of these plants have long since closed, some are still kicking and engaged in the kind of manly work that I will never remotely comprehend.

So that's the book, I guess. Did it seem like a book? Kind of? I don't know.

Who cares? It's done. And I guess if you're reading this it means they must have actually published it. Ha! Fuckin' A!

Now I don't want you guys thinking that just because I'm a big-time published author now that this success is going to go to my head. I'm still the same ol' down-to-earth, witty and debonair alpha male with a black belt in judo that I was before all of this happened. And that's never going to change.

But now does seem like a good time to announce that the movie rights for this book are officially for sale to the highest bidder. And if I have anything to say about the casting I would really like to see what Daniel Craig would do with the role of current-day Mike Polk, if we are able to schedule the shooting in between Bond films, obviously.

We'll get one of those irascible Culkin kids to play me as a child. And I of course will portray college-aged Mike Polk during the steamy soft-core scenes with my Kent State–era girlfriend Kendra (played by both Mila Kunis and Natalie Portman in a bold casting move).

But I'm getting ahead of myself. Right now, I'm just going to bask in the glory of this hastily made picture book full of locally-flavored humor so predictable that you really didn't even need to open it.

But I'm ever so glad you did! I've really enjoyed this time we've spent together and I thank you for deciding to purchase it from your local Dollar Tree instead of the unauthorized Andre Agassi biography that you were also considering. And by the way, you didn't miss anything. He practiced hard, got good at tennis, went super-bald, the end.

Thanks again kids. Take 'er easy. And Stay Cleveland Strong!

SOURCES

We took most of the pictures for this book ourselves. But we also used this open-use Wikipedia website for some stuff because we didn't want to have to find Ricky Davis and take a picture of him. So thanks to these faceless strangers whose pictures we used without them knowing it. And they'll probably never know it. But now it's good and legal. Rock on.

Bikini Girl - http://commons.wikimedia.org/wiki/File:Bikini_contest_-_black_bikini.jpg
Lamborghini - http://commons.wikimedia.org/wiki/File:SC06_2005_Lamborghini_Gallardo.jpg
Flag - http://commons.wikimedia.org/wiki/File:Flag_of_the_United_States.png
Grenade - http://commons.wikimedia.org/wiki/File:Hand_grenade_002.jpg
Double Guitar - http://commons.wikimedia.org/wiki/File:Ibanez_Studio_ST-1200BS_double_neck_electric_guitar.jpg
Great White Shark - http://commons.wikimedia.org/wiki/File:Whiteshark-TGoss1.jpg
Dortmunder - http://commons.wikimedia.org/wiki/File:Greatlakesdort.jpg
Bernie Kosar - http://commons.wikimedia.org/wiki/File:Greatlakesdort.jpg
Corned Beef - http://commons.wikimedia.org/wiki/File:Corn_beef_Reuben_sandwich.jpg
Trophy - http://commons.wikimedia.org/wiki/File:Althea_Gibson's_Wimbledon_Trophy_1956.jpg
Satin - http://commons.wikimedia.org/wiki/File:Satin_bedding.jpg
Ricky Davis - http://commons.wikimedia.org/wiki/File:Ricky_Davis_2007-12-30.jpg
Earth - http://upload.wikimedia.org/wikipedia/commons/0/07/537521main_earth_pacific_full.jpg
Gasoline - http://upload.wikimedia.org/wikipedia/commons/6/6e/HelenGeorgia1929Ford1975Gas.jpg
Pope - http://upload.wikimedia.org/wikipedia/commons/6/64/Paolovi.jpg
Internet - http://upload.wikimedia.org/wikipedia/commons/f/fe/CERN_NEXT_Server_2010-07-01.jpg
Sulu - http://upload.wikimedia.org/wikipedia/commons/f/f8/George_Takei_Sulu_Star_Trek.JPG
Julie Andrews - http://upload.wikimedia.org/wikipedia/commons/2/2a/Julie_Andrews_1970.JPG
Nixon - http://upload.wikimedia.org/wikipedia/commons/2/21/NIXONcampaigns.jpg
Betty White - http://upload.wikimedia.org/wikipedia/commons/d/d2/Betty_White_Georgia_Engel_Betty_White_Show_1977.JPG
Man on Moon - http://upload.wikimedia.org/wikipedia/commons/f/fe/Apollo_15_flag%2C_rover%2C_LM%2C_Irwin.jpg
Reagan - http://upload.wikimedia.org/wikipedia/commons/4/42/Ronald_Reagan_and_Nancy_Reagan_aboard_a_boat_in_California_1964.jpg
Runners - http://upload.wikimedia.org/wikipedia/commons/d/d1/Bundesarchiv_Bild_183-B0407-0013-003%2C_Berliner_Waldlaufmeisterschaften.jpg
Grenade - http://upload.wikimedia.org/wikipedia/commons/8/8c/Type_86P_grenade.jpg
Double-neck guitar - http://upload.wikimedia.org/wikipedia/commons/f/f0/SamboraKramerRSDouble.jpg
Eddie Money - http://upload.wikimedia.org/wikipedia/commons/7/75/Eddie-money-post-concert.jpg
Mayor Jackson - http://cgears.argoproject.org/files/2011/02/Mayor-Jackson-photo-by-Donn-R-Nottage.jpg

THANK YOUS!

So this is where I thank people and whatnot.

The awesome thing about my friends and family is that they're all totally used to the stupid crap that I'm always doing. So now when I call one of them and say that I need him to meet me in a public park in 25 minutes because I have to take a picture of him pretending to be John Elway, he doesn't even ask, "What for?," he just shows up and gets it over with.

I'm ridiculously fortunate to have so many wonderful and willing people around me, and here are the names of the ones that I'm not callously forgetting:

First, thanks to David Gray, Rob Lucas, and the entire Gray & Company staff for their infinite patience with a novice, man-child writer through egregiously missed deadlines and infinite nonsense. I also thank them for their reluctant acceptance of what was often entirely unnecessary profanity. Like this one: TWAT-KNOCKER!! (See? They printed that. And that's the kind of artistic freedom that I really appreciate.)

PEOPLE WHO I ABUSED TO GET THIS THING DONE:

(In no particular order but also non-alphabetical because I don't feel like doing that.)

Abby Dennstedt, Stephanie Remy, Britni Cartier, Rachel Peterson, Allison "Ally Woo" Hatton, Erin Wallace, Heather Martin, Chris "Dobber" Clem, Brian Mitchell, Matt Kane, Madman Marv Conner, Kirk Robinson, Owen Robinson, Tim Misny AAL, Marc Brown, Dick Goddard, Julia & Aaron Garmon, Mark McKenzie, Superhost, Matt Zitelli, Aaron McBride, Jim Fath, Chad Zumock, Big Chuck, HOT CARL!, Bill Squire, Home Team, Macduff, Michelle Burlingame, Drew Lisy, Dan Halloran, Ramon Rivas II, Korski Vodka, Evan Lang, Gargantuen, Brandon P. Davis, Jackie Greiner, Mary Smith, Kay Suzelis, Judy Prebish, Rev. Jim Rhoads, Katie McKee, Christian, Erin, Sadie & Shannon Dohar, Miss Katie Polk, Mike & Peggy Polk, Greg & Laurie McKee

I ABUSED THESE PEOPLE EXTRA SPECIAL HARD, SO THEY DESERVE EXTRA SPECIAL PROPS:

Jameson Campbell, Zachariah Durr & Jim Tews
for their guidance and exceptional graphic design work

&

Mike Beder
for always being the grownup in the room

Finally, this book was pretty much made by Chelsea McKee. She's listed as the graphic designer but she essentially did everything. So if you like it, thank her. And if you hate it, blame her. I spouted out a bunch of nonsense and she organized it and made it look like something. She endured high doses of me for a length of time that would make most people crumble, and for that alone she deserves several of the shiniest medals.

The fact that we made it out of this not only without becoming enemies but as better friends is a testament to either the strength of her character or the magnitude of her depravity. And even if we don't sell one goddamned book it was an unparalleled pleasure to work and drink alongside her. I wouldn't trade a minute of the madness. Love ya kid.

And . . .

THANK YOU, CLEVELAND!

—Mike Polk Jr.

FRAGILE!

CLEVELAND

UP